D0188571

THE ORIGIN OF CHINESE DEITIES

Cheng Manchao

FOREIGN LANGUAGES PRESS · BEIJING

First Edition 1995

Translated by
Chen Dezhen
Fang Zhiyun
Feng Huaxiu

ISBN 7-119-00030-6
© Foreign Languages Press, Beijing, 1995
Published by Foreign Languages Press
24 Baiwanzhuang Road, Beijing 100037, China

Printed by Beijing Foreign Languages Printing House
19 West Chegongzhuang Road, Beijing 100044, China

Distributed by China International Book Trading
Corporation
35 Chegongzhuang Xilu, Beijing 100044, China
P.O. Box 399, Beijing, China

Printed in the People's Republic of China

Foreword

The so-called god did not exist before the appearance of the human race. It gradually took shape as the human species multiplied. Men not only needed food and materials for survival, they also required a spiritual prop in their lives, thus creating the god. China, with a long history, has a rich tradition of creating gods. Innumerable gods, demons, immortals and spirits were created and spread far and wide among the people. This book selects twenty-nine Chinese gods to deal with, one by one.

Men desired peace. They wanted to win promotion and get rich, to achieve longevity and they hoped for a spouse to give birth to a son. As a result, they fabricated various ideas of gods and deities to provide sustenance in their illusions. A survey reveals that China had a wide spectrum of folk beliefs, including divinities, spirits, totems, prodigies, omens, divinations, taboos and sacrificial rites. Some of the gods dealt with in this book took their origin in men's worship of nature. As they could not explain many awesome and inspiring phenomena in the natural world, they began to worship these as supernatural beings. This gave rise to the existence of the gods of heaven, earth, fire, wind, rain, mountain and river. As human society developed, the ruler associated himself with the gods of the masses, creating the notion that the emperor had been invested by Heaven with the power to rule. Gods came in increasing numbers, with official titles, power, clothing, insignia of rank, and retinue, all similar to those used in the world of men. Finally, gods turned out to be everywhere and able to do everything. There was the Jade Emperor in Heaven, the King of Hell underground, the Dragon King in the water, the Village God, the Kitchen God, the Door God, the God of Wealth, the Mountain God, the City God and others. The god was not subjected to the natural law, but could exert profound influence over the human society. Both the authority of the sovereign and the religious authority simultaneously ruled the society. The gods discussed in this book were not all created by the ruler, nor were their titles granted by him. Some were outstanding personages who were deified after temples were built by the people to enshrine and honour them. These included Lu Ban, master founder of carpentry; Sun Simiao, King of Medicine, and hydraulic engineers Li Bing and his son. To these gods, especially at the initial stage, worshippers came to pay homage with more considerations to commemorate them than superstitious beliefs. Some other gods were neither worshipped by the masses, nor titled by the rulers. They were simply created by writers with a gifted pen, such as the Eight Immortals and Jiang Taigong.

As a matter of fact, the appearance of the gods and the custom of worshipping them reflect one aspect of China's "popular culture." This is because the faith in the deity is not only a religious phenomenon. It constitutes an important, integral part of Chinese folk culture and customs, exerting a widespread influence over China itself, overseas Chinese, and even Japan, Korea, Southeast Asia and the Malay Archipelago. It is helpful to explore the gods, from which one can see Chinese folk culture incorporate things of diverse nature. It preserved tradition while not rejecting foreign things providing they suited the taste of the local people. The study of folk beliefs is important to the study of archaeology, history, sociology, psychology, and folk literature.

Avalokitesvara—Saviour of All in Distress

Zhong Kui—the Ghost-Tamer

The God of Wealth

The Kitchen God

Door Gods

Lord Guan—the Demon-Subduer

The Dragon King

Goddess of Heaven—Goddess of the South China Sea

八仙過海

The Eight Immortals

CONTENTS

AVALOKITESVARA— SAVIOUR OF ALL IN DISTRESS

If you visit a Chinese temple or monastery, you will often see the image of Avalokitesvara. Wooden gilded statues of this Buddhist bodhisattva with a thousand eyes and hands are found in the Guangji (Universal Blessing) Temple of Beijing, the Guanyin Temple of Qinhuangdao, the Guanyin Hill of Yangzhou, and the Xiangguo (Grand Minister) Temple of Kaifeng. As the most popular deity among the Chinese people, he has been regarded as a saviour of all in distress, or a bestower of happiness. Legends represent him as a sage who upholds justice, drives out evil, bestows children on the childless and fortunes on the needy, and often appears in people's dreams exhorting them to do good works and abstain from doing evil. Many people believe these stories and enshrine his image in their homes for regular worship.

The Origin of Avalokitesvara

The Sanskrit term Avalokitesvara is translated into

Chinese as Guanshiyin, meaning "regarder (not hearer) of the world's sounds or cries." He is one of the triad of Amida and is represented on his left. Buddhist scriptures, based on Indian myths and legends, say that once two brothers were ordained into full monkhood and made the great vow of delivering all worldly beings. The two, so the story goes, became attendants of Amida Buddha; the elder one being called Avalokitesvara Bodhisattva and the younger one Mahasthama Bodhisattva, and the trio has since been known as "the three sages of the western quarter."

Folk tales and classical novels, such as *Journey to the West*, all describe Avalokitesvara, or Guanshiyin, as the most favoured of the bodhisattvas, a bodhisattva of great mercy and compassion, who is all-powerful and capable of incarnating in a thousand and one forms. The name of Guanshiyin was shortened to Guanyin after Mahayana Buddhism had spread to China in the Tang Dynasty (618-907).

Stories of Guanshiyin rescuing people from distress are found not only in written records and the random notes of scholars but also in official historical documents, such as the *History of the Northern Dynasties*. One said that after chanting the *Avalokitesvara-Sutra* a prisoner found his shackles gone and the ward-door thrown wide open; that a prisoner, Sun Jingde, of the Eastern Wei Dynasty (533-550) also chanted the sutra just before execution and when the executioner brought his knife down on him, it broke into three pieces. In ancient times, so another story goes, the *Raksha* (man-eating demon) often haunted the Lake Erhai and Cangshan Mountain regions in Yunnan Province in various forms, devouring people, especially the only child of a family. When Guanyin learned of this, he transformed himself into an old monk and subdued the demon. Out of gratitude to Guanyin for ridding the people of the scourge, they met and offered sacrifices to the god every year on his birthday.

Is Guanyin a Man or a Woman?

Many Buddhist paintings in the Mogao Grottoes in Dunhuang, Gansu Province, represent Guanyin as a male with a moustache. In the 500-volume *Taiping Miscellany*, edited by Li Fang and others of the Northern Song Dynasty (960-1126), and other books, Guanyin is also represented as a male. Buddhism, however, believes that all Buddhas and bodhisattvas are asexual supernatural beings that appear in various forms in different circumstances. According to Buddhist scriptures, there are thirty-two forms of Guanyin, sometimes—as found in Buddhist temples—with six faces, seven faces, thirty-two faces, or with a thousand hands and eyes. In the Southern and Northern Dynasties (420-589) Guanyin was represented sometimes as a male and sometimes as a female, whereas since the Tang

Dynasty the images of the bodhisattva have been those of a female figure. Even today, Guanyin is universally regarded as a beautiful woman. An explanation is called for.

According to the *History of the Northern Qi Dynasty* edited by the early-Tang Historian Li Baiyao, Emperor Wucheng (r. 561-564) of the Northern Qi Dynasty (550-577) once dreamed of Guanshiyin as a beautiful woman. Nobody knows whether the emperor had such a dream, but one thing is certain, Guanshiyin was represented as a female in the paintings by folk artists of the Southern and Northern Dynasties period.

In the eyes of Buddhist followers, Amida Buddha was ranked too high for them to communicate directly with him. As for the Buddhist followers of Han nationality, a bodhisattva in the company of the "patriarch of the western quarter" was needed, who knew the Han Chinese language and could keep Amida Buddha constantly posted on the suffering and the good deeds of the Han Chinese, so that he could give correct guidance to them. Consequently, both the nationality and sex of Avalokitesvara were completely changed to comply with the wishes of the Buddhist followers of the Han nationality.

During the Southern and Northern Dynasties, Buddhism spread swiftly in China and the number of nuns and female converts also increased by leaps and bounds. To meet women converts' wish for going to the "paradisc in the western quarter" after death, there appeared the "Avalokitesvara Bodhisattva, the Saviour of Great Compassion," or the so-called Goddess of Mercy. With the passage of time, people ceased to remember Avalokitesvara as the crown prince, Bushun (One Without Winking), of an Indian king, and the bodhisattva became an elegant woman in white, a cult for the women Buddhist converts.

In the Yuan Dynasty (1279-1368), an aristocrat, Madame Guan, printed a *Biography of the Goddess of Mercy*, in which she produced a pedigree of Avalokitesvara and tried in every way to prove the bodhisattva as the fair sex. Madame Guan and other aristocratic women believed that a female bodhisattva could perform certain tasks not fit for a male bodhisattva, such as the bestowing of children. The images of Guanyin found in Chinese temples in this period were more often than not those of a female figure. According to the *Notes and Sketches of Hu Yinglin*, more and more statues of Guanyin in the temples of the Northern Song period were represented as female. In the Southern Song period (1127-1279), most of the images of Guanyin were those of a pretty female figure "with crescent-shaped eyebrows, sparkling eyes, a jade-white smiling face and scarlet lips," wearing fringes, a brocade robe, her hair done in a bun at the back of her head, a willow wand in her right hand and a vase in her left hand.

5

Tales About the Thousand-Eye and Thousand-Hand Bodhisattva

Tales about Guanyin also changed with the appearance of the bodhisattva in female form. By the Northern Song Dynasty, many of the tales had been related to Chinese history. One said that she was Miao Shan, the third daughter of Prince Zhuang of Chu in the Spring and Autumn Period (722-481 B.C.), who started practising abstinence from meat and chanting Buddhist sutras from her childhood days. Later when she asked her father for permission to be ordained for nunhood, the prince flew into a rage and ordered her to kill herself with a sword. The sword did not hurt her; on the contrary, it broke into a thousand pieces. Then the prince had her throttled to death and her soul sent to the inferno, but the King of Hell brought her back to life on a lotus blossom in a pond on Mount Putuo on the East Sea outside Hangzhou Bay in Zhejiang Province. Legend has it that her birthday was the nineteenth day of the second lunar month, the date of her achievement of immortality was the nineteenth day of the sixth lunar month and the date of her attainment of nirvana was the nineteeth day of the ninth lunar month. After regaining her life, she started ridding human beings of their distress, restoring eyesight to the blind, curing people of their diseases, giving milk to cows, bestowing sons on eunuchs, finding husbands for spinsters, rescuing shipwreck victims, and other acts of benevolence.

Once when Prince Zhuang fell seriously ill, Miao Shan, unmindful of the wrongs her father had done her, saved him from the jaws of death by gouging out her own eyes and cutting off her own hands and making them into medicinal pills. To commemorate her and atone for his misdeeds, Prince Zhuang recruited all the master craftsmen in his state and asked them to make a statue of Guanyin with "*quan yan quan shou*" (meaning "intact eyes and hands"). The craftsmen, however, misheard it for "*qian yan qian shou*" (meaning "a thousand eyes and hands"). That is why many of the present images of Guanyin in the temples and monasteries are those with a thousand eyes and hands. The Octagonal Arhat Hall in the Xiangguo Temple in Kaifeng was built between 1766 and 1768 in the thirty-first to thirty-third year of the Qianlong reign period of the Qing Dynasty. Covering an area of seven hundred square metres, the architectural complex comprises a hall with covered corridors, a courtyard and a central pavilion—all octagonal in shape. In the pavilion is the statue of a thousand-eye and thousand-hand Avalokitesvara Bodhisattva, which is seven metres in height and weighing four tons. This gilt statue, with faces and hands in all four directions, making a total of 1,048 hands and 1,048 eyes, was done out of one gingko tree. This implies that she is quick of eye and deft of hand when delivering worldly beings.

The Bestower of Children and Wealth

This refers to the boy, Sudhana, standing on the left side of Avalokitesvara in Chinese temples and monasteries. This bodhisattva of the Buddhist faith is an instance of the possibility for one to attain Buddhahood through self-cultivation in this life, as preached by Mahayana Buddhism, instead of three lives (previous life, this life and after life). The practice of placing Sudhana on the left side of Avalokitesvara in the porch of the main gate to temples of the Zen sect is based on the story of Sudhana paying respects to fifty-three teachers and finally acknowledging Avalokitesvara as his teacher. This practice started in the Yuan Dynasty. Since then, Sudhana became the errand boy handling the bestowal of children and wealth by the Goddess of Mercy. Few people knew the myth which says that many treasures emerged automatically at the time of Sudhana's birth. They gathered that the boy must be good at managing money matters or good at making money, because "Sudhana" in Sanskrit and the Chinese translation, "Shancai," literally means "good at money." For this reason many rich merchants and landlords in the old days paid homage to Sudhana as a "God of Wealth." The vase and willow wand in Avalokitesvara's hands originally symbolized the bodhisattva spreading the dharma all over the world. Later, as they were described by some people as the talismans with which Avalokitesvara con-

trolled the weather, people in many areas would pray to the god for rain when there was a drought.

The Statue of Guanyin in Dule Temple

Inside the West Gate of Jixian County (ancient Yuyang) in the suburbs of Tianjin is Dule Temple, where a twenty-three-metre-high Guanyin Pavilion houses an exquisite sixteen-metre-high statue of Guanyin. The pavilion consists of three levels; the middle level, where the goddess is enshrined, is a vertical shaft, so that a visitor can see her from the floor on any level. For centuries Buddhist followers in the Jixian region have regarded the goddess as a mascot, offering sacrifices to her and making donations to the temple. A temple fair is held there in the third lunar month every year, when people flock to the temple praying to the bodhisattva for enlightening them to the ways of making money, ridding them of their distress and bestowing happiness, health and peace on them. In the past few years, Dule Temple has been refurbished to become a tourist attraction to the east of Beijing.

The exact date of construction of Dule Temple is unknown, although the celebrated architect Liang Sicheng (1901-1972) dated it back to the early Tang Dynasty at the latest. No Tang relics, however, have been handed down to posterity. The Guanyin Pavilion and the main gate were rebuilt in A.D. 984, in

the second year of the Tonghe period of the Liao Dynasty, while the monks' quarters and temporary residence for the emperor were constructed in the Ming and Qing dynasties. The last rebuilding of the temple took place in the twenty-sixth year of the Qing Emperor Guangxu's reign (1901), when the emperor and his retinue planned to stop over in the temple en route to the East Imperial Mausoleum at Zunhua County in Hebei Province to pay respects to the royal ancestors. Interesting relics of the temple include the handwriting of the emperor in the Guanyin Pavilion and a horizontal board on the main gate which bears three gilt Chinese characters for Dule Temple, believed to be in the calligraphy of the notorious prime minister Yan Song of the Ming Dynasty (1368-1644).

According to *Records of Dule Temple*, three massacres took place in Jixian in the Ming and Qing periods. At each massacre, thousands of Buddhist converts gathered in the temple area to protect "the sacred centre of the Jixian people, so that the temple remained intact, although the city was destroyed."

In the Qing period, Dule Temple was out of bounds to the common people and all the ceremonies during the annual fair could be held only in front of the temple. In the last years of the Qing Dynasty, a thief made a cozy home of the ceiling of the Guanyin Pavilion for a whole year. He went up and down the pavilion through the pillars on the east side of the building.

In 1928, when a warlord unit was stationed in Dule Temple, the main hall became its barracks. The commander of the unit, Sun Dianying, was also the culprit responsible for robbing the Empress Dowager Ci Xi's tomb in the East Imperial Mausoleum. While the mausoleum had been reduced to a mess, the temple had remained intact because it contained no gold, silver or other treasures.

In the eleventh lunar month of the fourteenth year of the Tianbao period in the Tang Dynasty (A.D. 755), when the An Lushan-Shi Siming Rebellion broke out in Yuyang, the rebel chief, An Lushan, held an oath-taking rally in Dule Temple. It is said that Dule Temple had previouly been called Avalokitesvara Bodhisattva Temple, before An Lushan, obsessed with the desire to become an emperor and have all the worldly pleasures to himself, renamed it as Dule (meaning "solitary happiness") on the eve of his rebellion.

ZHONG KUI—
THE GHOST-TAMER

*I*n the old days, the picture of Zhong Kui was posted on the walls of almost all Chinese homes. He was represented as a fierce warrior with the head of a leopard and an imposing figure, wearing whiskers, a long robe, a pair of boots, and pointing his sword at a ghost under his feet. Posting such a picture in one's home, according to tradition, would protect it from disasters and prolong one's life.

Tales About Zhong Kui Taming Ghosts

According to *Notes Written in Dream*, written by Shen Kuo of the Song Dynasty, once when Emperor Xuanzong (r. 712-756) of the Tang Dynasty was returning from reviewing his troops at Lishan on the outskirts of Xi'an, he suffered an attack of malaria. He was confined to bed for more than a month, despite efforts of the imperial physicians and witches to cure him. One night he dreamed of two demons. The smaller one, clad in a red robe with an apron round his waist, one foot in a boot

and the other foot bare, was running away with the purple perfume-sachet of the emperor's favoured concubine, Lady Yang, and the emperor's own white jade flute which he had just stolen. The bigger demon, wearing a felt hat, a blue robe and a silk ribbon round his waist but no shoes on his feet, his sleeves rolled up, seized the little demon, gouged out his eyes and devoured him. When the emperor asked him who he was, the bigger demon replied, "I am Zhong Kui of Zhongnan. I killed myself after I had failed in the examination for the selection of military officers, and I have vowed to exterminate all demons in the world for Your Majesty's sake." When the emperor awoke to find his ailment cured, he ordered the court painter Wu Daozi to paint a picture of Zhong Kui in the image or the ghost-tamer he saw in his dream. In addition, he issued an edict to the whole nation, ordering the picture of Zhong Kui hung in people's homes on New Year's Eve so as to "drive away the ghosts and purify the evil atmosphere."

The *Universal Joy* by Zhang Dafu of the Qing Dynasty notes, "In the Tang Dynasty, there lived a man named Zhong Kui in Zhongnan, who was a diligent student from a very poor family. In the year of a triennial national civil examination, with financial support by kind-hearted neighbours, he went to the capital and passed the examination with honours. In an interview given to the successful candidates, Emperor Dezong was displeased with the ugly looks of Zhong Kui and divested him of his title. Zhong Kui died of a broken heart and, when his spirit drifted to hell, he poured forth his grievances to the King of Hell. Moved by his uprightness, the King of Hell memorialized the Jade Emperor in Heaven, who appointed Zhong Kui as Ghost-Taming General. Henceforth, Zhong Kui became a deity "in command of ghosts."

As a matter of fact, the name of Zhong Kui underwent many changes. It appeared as far back as the Six Dynasties Period (from the early third to the late sixth century). Later, parents started to give their new-born babies names homophonic with that of Zhong Kui, in the hope that they would scare away evil spirits and grow up strong and healthy or live to be a hundred years old. By the Tang Dynasty, people had drawn a forced analogy from the tales about Zhong Kui and turned him from a guardian god against evil spirits into one capable of taming and devouring ghosts and demons—the evil forces in the human world. There are several forms of writing for the name of Zhong Kui, all of which are somewhat homophonic with the Chinese character for cudgel (*zhui*). The scholar Gu Yanwu of the Ming-Qing period said in his Records of Daily Knowledge that this originated from the fact that the ancient Chinese used a *zhui* to ward off ghosts and demons.

Zhong Kui Tames the Ghosts

What were the ghosts that Zhong Kui was out to exterminate? The answer to this question is found in a memorial the Kings of Ten Hells presented to the Jade Emperor: "As administrators of the nether world, your humble subjects feel duty bound to pass unbiased verdicts on all crimes. However, there are strange demi-ghosts in the Tang Empire in the southern land, who have the motives for committing crimes but on whom, having no evidence for their crimes, we cannot administer the royal law. For this reason, the world is dark and right is confused with wrong. Your humble subjects have been gripped by worries. Fortunately, we can now count on Zhong Kui...." What Zhong Kui is out to do away with are just demons in the human world, such as sycophants, drunkards, double-dealers, swindlers, and lechers.

The following are records of how Zhong Kui tamed ghosts.

The first ghost Zhong Kui tackled was Arrogant Ghost. As soon as Zhong Kui and his party arrived at the human world and took up their lodging in an ancient temple, a demon came to visit Maitreya Buddha with a letter of introduction. When Zhong Kui reproved him for his bad manners, the demon retorted, "If I tell you who I am, you will know I am a person who ought to be invited to a seat of honour while you should stand in waiting on the side." He claimed to be a fellow-disciple with Maitreya Buddha learning the Tao (the Way) from the same tutor. "Then I was appointed Grand General Equalling Heaven," he continued, "a general next to nobody in rank, with power over Heaven and Earth. When the Great Heavenly Emperor sees me, he addresses me as 'Your Excellency my teacher,' and when the Kings of Ten Hells fall across me, they present themselves to me as 'Your humble subordinates so and so.'" Zhong Kui told the demon to go back and bring his weapon for a fight. In a trice the demon vanished in the sky. Appalled at his supernatural power, Zhong Kui consulted with his two subordinate generals for a way to deal with the demon. Fu Qu, the Trail-Blazing General, said he had wondered why the demon should pay respects to the clay idol of Maitreya Buddha and why the name of the demon had not been found on the "Register of Ghosts and Demons." At this, Zhong Kui ordered another general, Han Yuan (The Wronged), to go and investigate in the guise of a country doctor. Han Yuan met an old man called Tong Feng (Informant) who was on his way to look for a doctor to cure his sick daughter, and the old man told him the demon was called Arrogant Ghost whose gold crown and garments were both borrowed. Zhong Kui laughed when Han Yuan reported the results of his investigations. Soon after, Arrogant Ghost arrived with a troop of ghost soldiers and challenged Zhong Kui to fight a duel. Zhong

Kui emerged from his formation and shouted, "Isn't that the Arrogant Ghost?" Arrogant Ghost was stunned, wondering how his adversary had come to know his name. When they were tied at the fiftieth round of fighting, the old man Tong Feng rushed on the scene. "Arrogant Ghost, give me back my garments," he yelled. "Your concubine has died of hunger and you are expected to run home to buy a coffin for her." Arrogant Ghost collapsed with fear. Zhong Kui gouged out his eyes, and from then on, the ghost had gone about shorn of his arrogant air.

Another story has it that once a county magistrate and Zhong Kui read a written complaint lodged by Lie-Telling Ghost, accusing someone of robbing his property in broad daylight and killing countless numbers of people. "Can you give me facts to support your complaint about the accused killing countless numbers of people?" asked the magistrate. Lie-Telling Ghost replied, "If my money and property had not been robbed, I could have used it to buy myself a wife and a bevy of concubines. Then they would give me several sons, who, when grown up, would marry and have sons and grandsons and so on to infinity. With my money and property gone, I am impoverished and will soon starve to death. Then I would leave no offspring behind. Doesn't this mean killing countless numbers of people?" Enraged by his absurd arguments, the magistrate was about to put him to torture, when Zhong Kui emerged from behind the screen and, brandishing his sword, cut off the liar's head with one fell swoop.

There were times, however, when Zhong Kui landed in trouble. One story tells how his leg was pulled by five ghosts. After Zhong Kui had killed Drunkard and driven Dandy into a coffin, Swindler cried and made up his mind to avenge them. So he got his ghost-brothers together and, when the county magistrate was away from the yamen on a mission, they entered the county yamen disguised as yamen runners. Seeing Zhong Kui sitting idly under a huge pine tree in the rear garden of the mansion, they went up to him, entertaining him with singing and dancing and plying him with drain after drain of liquor until he was inebriated. Swindler removed Zhong Kui's boots from his feet; Scapegoat took off his sword and Philanderer took away his scepter, while Shortlived Ghost climbed up the tree and fished up his official gauze cap with one foot. When General Fu Qu returned and saw Swindler leaving with the boots on his back, he captured him and the other ghosts. He was wondering where the gauze cap had disappeared, when he heard the rustle of the tree leaves and saw Shortlived Ghost shivering on the branch, the gauze cap on his head. He shot the demon down with an arrow, picked up the cap and put it on Zhong Kui's head. Only then did Zhong Kui wake up. When he saw his two guardian generals and found what had happened, he felt embarrassed and pledged that he would give up drinking and eliminate all the ghosts and monsters on earth.

The Impact of Zhong Kui's Ghost-Taming on Posterity

The tales about Zhong Kui's taming and devouring ghosts became current in the Tang Dynasty, when Emperor Xuanzong ordered the pictures of Zhong Kui hung at the end of a year. By Dezong's reign in the mid-Tang period, the emperor made it a point to bestow calendars with pictures of Zhong Kui on the courtiers on New Year's Eve. During the Song Dynasty, the common people hung pictures of Zhong Kui on the Double Fifth Day and New Year's Eve as a shield against evil spirits. The enshrining of Zhong Kui as a deity is not only because he was praised by the feudal rulers, but also because of his wide representation in literary works and the graphic arts. The most popular in this regard are the Ming Dynasty's *Stories of Taming Ghosts* by Yanxia Sanren, *Records of the Taming of Ghosts* by Taoist priest Yun Zhong, and *Story of Zhong Kui Marrying Off His Younger Sister*; Qing Dynasty's paintings *Portrait of Zhong Kui* by famous painter Dong Shen, *The Drunken Zhong Kui* by Luo Pin, and *Zhong Kui Marries Off His Younger Sister* by Hua Yan; and the modern Chinese painting *Drinking Zhong Kui* by master painter Xu Beihong.

THE GOD OF WEALTH

People worship the God of Wealth because they want to live a happy, affluent life. Every year on the Spring Festival (Lunar New Year), every family makes a practice of welcoming the God of Wealth and offering sacrifices to him, before members of the family gather together for a feast of jiaozi (dumplings with meat and stuffing, shaped like a *yuanbao*, a gold or silver ingot). Jiaozi is said to be the "*yuanbao* given by the God" and it is believed that when one ushers in the God of Wealth and eats the *jiaozi*, fortune, happiness and wealth will come his way. On New Year's Eve, every household welcomes the God of Wealth in the direction pointed by the traditional almanac. At midnight, someone will announce outside, "I have brought you the God of Wealth!" At this, the woman of the house will reward the courier with a *doubao* (dumpling stuffed with sweetened bean paste). In return she will receive a slip of paper that augurs good fortune.

The God of Wealth, a member of the Taoist pantheon, is one of the most popular deities with the Chinese people of all walks of life. The god, however, varies from period to period, and from place to place. In modern times, there have been legends about a God of Wealth with a civil mien and a God of Wealth with military bearing. Of all the Gods of Wealth, the best-known has been Zhao Gongming, alias Zhao Xuantan. There are also two legends about this deity. One, based on the *Feng Shen Yan Yi* (*Romance of the Canonized Gods*), a novel by Xu Zhonglin of the Ming Dynasty (1368-1644), says that a person named Zhao Gongming once made his home in Luofu Cave on Mount Emei, cultivating himself according to Taoist doctrines. After he had attained the Tao, he acquired an immortal frame, extraordinary military skills, a black tiger as his mount and an iron rod as his weapon, complete with two talismans—a Sea-Calming Pearl and a Dragon-Tying Rope. Then King Zhou of the Shang Dynasty sent for him to help fight Jiang Ziya, the field marshal of King Wen of the Zhou Dynasty. In the battle to break through Jiang Ziya's "Ten-Impasse Formation," Zhao Gongming inflicted a disastrous defeat on Jiang Ziya. Because Zhao had assisted the tyrant King Zhou in oppressing the people, he was shot to death by arrows. Afraid lest the spirit of the departed should try to seek revenge, the victorious field marshal honoured Zhao Gongming with the title of God of Wealth. The *Random Notes of Yingkou* by Zhu Anren of the Qing Dynasty explains: "People extend their New Year greetings first of all to the God of Wealth—a gilt or coloured image of an eight-foot-

21

tall man, flanked by the Wealth Usher on the left and the Treasure Carrier on the right." This refers to the God of Wealth held up by rich people and wealthy merchants—a deity with a dark face, bushy whiskers, and iron helmet on his head and an iron rod in one hand, sitting astride a black tiger.

The other legend is about the Taoist deity Zhao Xuantan, popularly known as Lord Zhao the Marshal. The *Compendium of the Deities of Three Religions*, Volume 3, says, "Lord Zhao the Marshal is named Zhao Lang, alias Zhao Gongming, a native of Zhongnan Mountain. During the Qin Dynasty (221-207 B.C.), he made his home in a mountain-girt region, where he cultivated himself according to Taoist doctrines. Upon completion of his cultivation, he was appointed Vice-Marshal of the Divine Heaven by the Jade Emperor. He wore an iron helmet on his head, held an iron rod in his hand, his face dark, his whiskers bushy, and rode around on a black tiger. He had control of thunder and lightning, wind and rain, and protected people from diseases and plagues. He upheld justice and redressed mishandled cases and bestowed wealth on pedlars and merchants as well as the needy. For this reason, he was honoured with the title "Marshal Zhao, the Tiger-Riding, Golden-Wheel Wielding Law Enforcer in Overall Control of the Heavenly Palace." Also, when Celestial Tutor Zhang Daoling asked for a guardian god to stand guard when he made elixir pills for immortality, the Jade Emperor appointed

Zhao Gongming as "Marshal of the Heavenly Palace to assist the Celestial Tutor in dispelling diseases, plagues and other disasters."

The above two legends tell about two deities of the same name, but the birthday and era of one are different from the birthday and era of the other. This indicates that the two stories—in fact, all the stories—of Zhao Gongming are fictitious. Moreover, no history books have ever touched upon canonization of the gods by Jiang Ziya or mentioned any person named Zhao Gongming.

In *Wits and Humour*, written by Wu Yanren of the Qing Dynasty and annotated by Lu Shudu, there is mentioned the Starlord of Wealth, also known as the Venus or the Gold Star. Some people say the God of Wealth is the Great Sage Equalling Heaven; some say the God of Wealth is the Wealth Usher; others say he is the Difang Ghost. Difang Ghost is one of two paper deities standing on either side of the altar for idolatrous thanksgiving service, who wears a mourning costume, a threadbare palm-leaf fan in one hand, a dunce-cap inscribed with the words "You will make a fortune at sight of me" on his head, bloody tears trickling from his eyes (the other being Mahasattva with a green face, long teeth, an iron chain in his hands, eyes protruding and stomach drawn in).

The God of Wealth has been the most popular of any deity in China. People pay respects to him, hoping that he will lift them out of humble circumstances or make them wealthy.

The following legend has been current among the people.

Beside the statue of the God of Wealth in the main hall of the City God Temple in Shanghai, there used to be an elegant female bodhisattva, the God of Wealth's wife. The two were devoted to each other, living a life of wealth on the endless sacrificial offerings from the worldly beings. One night, a pilgrim in rags entered the hall and prayed to the God of Wealth for his blessings. Seeing the pilgrim was a beggar, the god frowned and turned his head away in displeasure. The beggar was not to be discouraged. For several months he came to the hall to pay homage to the God of Wealth. One day he came stumbling into the hall, but he collapsed on the floor before he had time to make a sacrificial offering. Seeing this, the female bodhisattva nudged her dozing husband and urged him to show pity on the beggar. Then she secretly plucked off a gold hairpin from her bun and threw it to the poor man. The flash of the gold hairpin woke the beggar from his swoon to find the precious object in his hand. Overjoyed, he made three mighty kowtows to the statues. The noise roused the God of Wealth from his sleep. When he saw what had happened, the God of Wealth flew into a rage. "So you are throwing money away to no purpose! Get out of my sight, you squanderer!" In this way, she was divorced. That's why visitors cannot find the image of the female bodhisattva in Shanghai's City God Temple today.

The poor people living in the vicinity of the temple have long since ceased to pay respects to the snobbish God of Wealth.

THE KITCHEN GOD

The Kitchen God, also known as the Kitchen King or Kitchen Lord, was respected and worshipped by emperors and commoners alike. It is said the god as an envoy was sent by the Jade Emperor in Heaven to every household in the mundane world to be the "master of the household" responsible for cooking and fuel. His duties, however, were not limited. He had to record from time to time people's merits and misdeeds and return to Heaven every year on the twenty-third day of the twelfth lunar month to report to the Jade Emperor. The Jade Emperor would give punishments to evil-doers and rewards to kind-hearted people.

Legends About the Kitchen God

There are many legends about offering sacrifices to the Kitchen God. In the old society before the Spring Festival, each household prayed to the Kitchen God, hoping that he would "put in a good word for the whole family when in the heavens and bless them when on earth." They thought the whole household would then live peacefully in the coming new year. Many people got along cautiously and behaved themselves well in order to make the Kitchen God bring them blessings. As time went by, it was discovered that poor people, respecting the Kitchen God piously, never got rewarded; while the rich people's lives got better and better only because of their good offerings. Then the commoners believed that the Kitchen Lord surely liked to hear good words and receive bribes just like officialdom in the human world. Later people added a kind of malt sugar shaped like a melon in their offerings to the Kitchen God in the hope of sticking up the god's teeth and keeping his mouth shut when he went back to Heaven.

The custom of sacrifices differed in various places. Some places held two sacrifices: one on the evening of the twenty-third day of the twelfth lunar month, with offerings including chicken, duck, fish, meat dishes and wine; the other on the next evening with fruit, peanuts, melon seeds, day lily and cakes. Malt sugar was a must in any sacrifices. The first sacrifice was meant to bribe the Kitchen God, hoping that he would not bring trouble to the worshippers. Purpose of the second sacrifice was to make the god clear-headed after the first evening's good food and wine; thus he would not talk irresponsibly in Heaven.

Offering sacrifices to the Kitchen God was unique in the national minority areas. The Zhuangs in

Guangxi made four sacrifices from the first to the fifteenth day of the first lunar month. They prayed for protection from eye disease and scabies. These were called "Kitchen King Sacrifices," and were divided into grand and minor sacrifices. The former's offerings included a piglet and a rooster and a sorcerer would be invited to take part in the grand sacrifice; the minor sacrifice had only half a kilo of pork and a rooster as the offering and no sorcerer was to take part. Women had to go away from home on both sacrifices, otherwise, the legend says, the Kitchen God would not dare come out to take offerings.

The Truth About the Kitchen God

The origin of worshipping the Kitchen God was rather complicated but time-honoured. As it was regarded to be closely related with people's food, drink and daily life just like land, wells, houses and roads, it naturally became a matter of worship. Sacrifice to the Kitchen God was listed as one of the state sacrificial ceremonies in *The Book of Rites* which collected records about etiquette and customs before the Qin Dynasty.

Who is the Kitchen God? Many legends about it can be found in Chinese history. Some say it was a man; some say a woman. The same is true of his family names. But Zhang might be his family name.

Why did people fabricate a Kitchen God? The fact is that people of primitive society wanted to show their gratitude to the inventor of fire so they held a special sacrifice to him every summer. It was said that summer symbolized fire and so did the kitchen. Legends about the Kitchen God can be traced to the Yin (Shang) Dynasty (c. 16th-11th century B.C.), when the diety was represented as an old lady responsible for food and drinks. Some ancient books describe the Kitchen God as "a beautiful young woman in red." Some books say, "There are red-shell worms the size of a cicada on the kitchen ranges, which are popularly called roach or *zao ma* (kitchen range horse)." In Sichuan Province, the roach is called "oil-stealing granny." Ancient people regarded it as a divine being. This, probably, is the origin of the Kitchen God.

After the Han Dynasty (206 B.C.-A.D. 220), the Kitchen God became a male deity. Sacrifice to him was then just a commemoration with little superstitious colour. The formation of a class society had injected new content into it, and legends about the Kitchen God were closely associated with money-making. One legend said that, during the reign of the Han Dynasty's Emperor Xiandi (91-49 B.C.), the Kitchen God suddenly appeared in the morning on the eighth day of the twelfth month when a man called Yin Yufang started cooking his meal. The man had a yellow sheep, which he slaughtered and offered as a sacrifice to the Kitchen God. From then on he had good luck at every turn and quickly became rich. He built himself a big, elaborate house and bought five thousand hectares of land. His family members lived lives of luxury, dressed in silk, ate nice food, and were waited upon by servants at home and travelled by carriage and riding on horses. His two grandsons both became high-ranking officials. The story about the Yins caught people's attention, especially those who yearned for wealth and position, touching off a craze for offering sacrifices to the Kitchen God.

In the meantime, many tales circulated about the Kitchen God. One said that at the end of every month the Kitchen God would ascend to Heaven to inform the Jade Emperor of the crimes committed by so-and-so on earth (see *Huai Nan Bi Wan Shu,* or *The Ten Thousand Infallible Arts of the Prince of Huainan*). Another said the Kitchen God and his wife were named so-and-so and they had six daughters. As time went on, the Kitchen God became empowered not only to take charge of a family's food and drink but also to control life and death, fortune and misfortune. He kept a regular register of one's good and bad deeds and reported them to the Jade Emperor once a year.

In order to preserve the feudal system and put the people at their beck and call, the feudal rulers concocted many stories about the Kitchen God being the arbiter of people's destiny. According to *Bao Pu Zi (The Book of Master Baopu),* when the

Kitchen God reported people's crimes to him, the Jade Emperor would punish the criminals by reducing their life span by three hundred to three days as he saw fit. In other words, if one wished to live long, one would have to behave according to the ethical codes of the time. In fact, people who believed in the existence of deities would never dare to offend the Kitchen God and always held him in esteem in the hope that he would put in a good word for them when in the heavens and bless them when on earth. Each month on the first and the fifteenth, people had to make offerings to him, and on the day whan the Kitchen God was said to be going back to Heaven for consultations, the offerings would have to be extravagant, including fish, meat, wine and sugar. Thus, the more bribes one gave the Kitchen God, the more good words the latter would allegedly put in for him. It was believed that those who could not afford such offerings would always be in for trouble. These legends, of course, represent only the wishes and yearnings of the people.

The legends about the Kitchen God are contradictory because ancient people could not explain many things in the natural world and therefore believed everything was controlled by some divine beings in the unseen world. The fact that the Kitchen God turned from female to male indicated that human society had developed from a matriarchal to a patriarchal society. As times changed, people's imagination also changed and so did the deities concocted by them out of thin air.

The Kitchen God became more and more powerful and ascended to Heaven frequently to report on people in the mundane world. The ruler used the deities to frighten the people and bind them to his will.

Beating the Kitchen King

However, not all people in ancient times believed in the existence of supernatural beings. A local opera, *Beating the Kitchen King*, throws some light on this. It tells about a poor man, who, having no way out, lived as a beggar. In the twelfth lunar month, he disguised himself as the Kitchen God and begged for money and food everywhere like a clown, for which he was often given a severe beating. A famous scholar in the Tang Dynasty once wrote an article refuting the tale about the Kitchen King going up to Heaven.

The following is another interesting popular story about how the Kitchen King was regarded by people.

Once there was a king who wished to taste all the nice food in the world. Everyday he asked his ministers to go and find good food for him. After some time, he got tired of everything his ministers offered. So he started on a tour to hunt for something unusual to eat. One day, he saw a beautiful girl, who was transformed from a fairy. She had been betrothed to a cowherd. Seeing a basket over her arm, the king said with a smile, "What is in your basket?" The girl replied, "It's jujube cakes." Though the king had eaten many choice foods, he had never heard of or eaten jujube cakes. So he asked the girl to share her cakes with him. When she handed him the basket, the king devoured all the cakes right there. Then he wanted the girl to marry him, so that she could make him such cakes whenever he wanted them. When his proposal was turned down, he deliberately made things difficult for her by asking her to make a hundred seventy-seven and one-half cakes, on pain of carrying her off. The girl promptly took off her golden hairpin, and with a stroke there appeared the exact number of cakes, and piping hot at that! Seeing the girl had not been overcome by his trick, he ordered her to feed him those cakes. This time, the girl refused. A busybody of an old woman came forward and urged the girl to comply with his request. When they tried to force her, the girl gave them each a resounding blow to the face, flipping them both behind the kitchen range. Pointing to them, the girl said, "You greedy creatures should always stand there watching while people eat." After that, the two have stood rooted behind the kitchen range. A colour woodblock print of the Kitchen King is still popular among the people, and it is based on this tale.

DOOR GODS

*D*oor Gods, as the name implies, are two deities standing guard over the door. Posting Door God pictures was a popular custom observed in ancient China. However, nobody can tell who the Door Gods are. Some say they are Zhong Kui and Yu Lei; others say they are Qin Qiong and Yuchi Gong; still others say they are Generals Wen and Yue. Some have said Door Gods are just Door Gods and that painting two brave warriors on the door is all right, but who cares who they are?

Pictures of Door Gods were nailed on the doors to ward off evil spirits. In the remote past, people offered sacrifices, like they did to the Kitchen God, mainly to show their respect for the creators of the houses, doors and windows for providing shelter against the elements, beasts and enemies.

Many records about Door Gods can be found in ancient Chinese classics. The following story had a great influence among the common people.

Long, long ago, there was a large peach forest on Dushuo Mountain in the centre of a sea. Two brothers, Shen Tu and Yu Lei, lived in a stone house under a large peach tree. Both were honest and upright, and both were men of unusual strength so that ferocious beasts such as lions, wolves and tigers all stayed away from them in fear. The small peaches in the tree were fragrant and sweet; the large ones, when eaten, were said to be able to turn people into immortals or deities.

Northeast of the mountain was Wild Ox Ridge, on which lived a vicious Wild King who often ate the hearts and drank the blood of the local people. When he heard that one could become immortal after eating the large peaches on Dushuo Mountain, he sent one of his men there to get him some of the peaches. But the two brothers refused and said, "Our peaches are for the poor, not for any king or emperor." So saying, they drove the man out.

Hearing this, the king flew into a rage and went up the mountain with three hundred soldiers. The two brothers with their guardian tigers engaged them in a fierce fighting. The king was defeated and fled in panic.

Back in Wild Ox Ridge, the king worked on a scheme to get his revenge.

On a windy, pitch-black night, when the brothers were sleeping in their stone house, they heard a loud noise outside. They opened the door to face scores of green-faced and long-toothed demons. Undaunted, the elder brother broke off a peach branch and the younger brother took some reed ropes and together they went to meet the demons. The elder brother grabbed one demon after another, while the younger one bound them up one by one and fed them all to the tigers.

These demons were all the king's men in disguise. The news spread far and wide the next day. People were grateful to the brothers for getting rid of the evil spirits. Then the brothers' names became known by more and more people. The legend says that after their death, they became immortals and lived in the Heavenly Palace. The Heavenly Lord then entrusted them both with the task of eliminating all demons that came their way. Whenever they met a demon, they just bound him hand and foot and fed him to tigers. It was said that as they lived in the peach forest, so peachwood could exorcize devils, too. Henceforth, common people all placed peachwood tallies inscribed with the names of Shen Tu and Yu Lei on either side of their gates to dispel evil spirits and bring peace to the family. Some people had pictures of the two brothers drawn and posted on their gates to become "Door Gods."

In the Tang Dynasty, people regarded Qin Shubao and Yuchi Gong as Door Gods. According to *Deities of Three Religions*, once when Emperor Taizong (r. 627-649) fell ill, he dreamed of ghosts howling and throwing bricks at him. In the war to found the Tang Dynasty, he had killed many people. So in his dream he saw many ghosts asking him to give back their lives. The emperor was frightened and woke up in a cold sweat. Then his two brave generals, Qin Shubao and Yuchi Gong, put on their armour and stood guard on either side of the palace gate, thus ensuring a peaceful night for the emperor. The emperor then asked a court painter to draw a picture of each of the two generals to hang on both sides of the palace gate. Common people then followed this practice to dispel evil spirits and handed it down to posterity. This was the origin of the Door Gods. The pictures of Shen Tu and Yu Lei, like Qin Shubao and Yuchi Gong, were also painted in the style of warriors so as to scare away demons.

The images of the Door Gods were mostly based on the Four Heavenly Kings in the temples. They were the four heavenly dharma protectors of Buddhism. They originated from the Indian mythological "Four Heavenly Kings to protect the world in the four directions of east, west, south and north." The kings were mostly buckled in their armour, with thick waists, holding a sword or an iron staff and standing on guard with an angry look. In some places, people simply used exorcizing inscriptions instead of Door God pictures. According to records, in 1119, during the Northern Song Dynasty, the Door Gods in the national capital of Kaifeng all wore tiger-head armour and held a spear standing guard at the gates of the houses of the princes. During the Shaoding reign (1228-1233) of the Southern Song Dynasty (1127-1279), pictures issued by Emperor Lizong (r. 1225-1264) became those of Zhong Kui. In the Ming and Qing dynasties, Door Gods varied in different places. The Door God pictures in Xinxiang, Henan, included brave generals of the Three Kingdoms Period, such as Zhao Yun (?-229) and Ma Chao (176-222), and a Taoist priest named Ran Deng. In the Hanzhong area of Shaanxi, the pictures of Sun Bin, a strategist of the Warring States Period, and some others were posted as Door Gods. In the period of the Qing Dynasty, Emperor Qianlong (r. 1736-1795), pictures of Door Boys instead of Door Gods were posted at Yangliuqing, the town famous for its New Year pictures. In *Records of Xiangfu County*, it is said that Door God pictures produced at Zhuxian Town were all images of generals or court officials, complete with pictures of bats and other insects traditionally symbolizing auspiciousness.

ZHANG XIAN—
THE SON-BESTOWER

In the old society, many women often prayed to Zhang Xian (meaning "Zhang the Immortal") to bestow sons on them. The origin of the Son-Bestowing Deity is strange. He is represented not by a clay or wooden statue but by the picture of a nobleman with a catapult under his arm in a hunting pose.

Sacrifice to Zhang Xian started in the Northern Song Dynasty (960-1132). Su Xun of the Song Dynasty and Gao Qi of the Ming both wrote poems on the paintings of Zhang Xian. Because his wife had not borne him a son many years after their marriage, Su Xun prayed to Zhang Xian the first thing every morning, and sure enough his wife later gave birth to a son for him. The following is a story of the origin of Zhang Xian as a Son-Bestowing Deity.

During the Five Dynasties Period (907-960), Meng Zhixiang, who founded the Later Shu Kingdom in Chengdu, Sichuan, died only a year after he became king. His son, Meng Chang, succeeded to the throne, but he cared nothing about state affairs, indulging in hunting and playing ball games. In 965, Emperor

Zhang Xian—the Son-Bestower

The Son-Bestowing Goddess

Taizu of the Song Dynasty dispatched General Wang Quanbin to attack the Later Shu. Meng was defeated and surrendered to the Song. He was taken to Bianjing (now Kaifeng, Henan Province), the Song capital, and was granted the title of the Duke of Qin. He died soon afterwards. His concubine, Madame Huarui, was taken into the Song palace. Missing her husband, she painted a portrait of Meng Chang with a catapult under his arm and hung it up in her room. When asked who the man was, she said it was a deity who would give sons to anyone who worshipped him. One day, when Emperor Taizu saw the picture and asked the same question, Madame Huarui told him the same story. When he asked about the deity's name, she told him casually that he was Zhang Xian, to whom all Shu people offered sacrifices. The following day, when the emperor visited her again, he ordered her to write a poem, with the downfall of the state of Later Shu as the theme. Madame Huarui dashed off a poem which read: "When the sovereign hoisted the white flag atop the city wall/His consort living in the narrow palace confines knew nothing about it./Fourteen hundred thousand soldiers all removed their armour./Not a single one of them could call himself a man." After reading the poem, the emperor made some casual remarks and left. Thus Zhang Xian became known as a son-bestower and worship of him as such spread from the palace to the men in the street. In fact, Zhang Xian was a male noble with a bow under his arm instead of a god.

Afterwards, some Taoist priests and superstitious people drew a forced analogy from the story, alleging that Zhang Xian was also called Zhang Yuanxiao, who had attained the Tao (the Way) on Qingcheng Mountain in Sichuan during the Five Dynasties Period. Some Qing Dynasty records say, "One day, an old man came to Zhang Yuanxiao with a bamboo catapult and three iron pellets and asked Zhang to give him three hundred coins. Without a second thought, Zhang gave him the money he asked for. The old man said, 'My pellets can dispel epidemics, so you should treasure them.' Later, the old man visited him again and imparted to him the Taoist way of salvation. Zhang found that there were two pupils in each of the old man's eyes. Years later, when Zhang visited the White Crane Mountain and saw a stone statue of an old man with four eyes, it dawned on him that the statue was nobody but the old man."

This story implied that Zhang Yuanxiao was not an immortal, but a mortal, who bought a catapult and pellets from an old man and learned the skill of using the weapon. In Meixian County, Sichuan, stands the former site of Zhang Yuanxiao's house. Zhang was already a famous catapult shooter as a youth, who often killed fierce beasts with this weapon. After his death, the local people made a painting of him with a catapult under his arm to cherish his memory. The character *dan* (pellet) has the same pronunciation as the character for birth and is similar in shape to the character for immortal. Some Taoist priests, therefore, announced that Zhang Yuanxiao had become an immortal. Because Meng Chang had been known as a son-bestower, Zhang also became a Son-Bestowing Deity. Tales about Zhang having attained the Tao and finally becoming an immortal were spread far and wide to verify his position as a Son-Bestowing Deity. With the spread of these tales, the painting of Meng Chang with a catapult under his arm turned into a painting of Zhang Xian, and more temples were set up in commemoration of Zhang Xian, attracting large numbers of people to worship him in the hope of having sons. The great poet Lu You (1125-1210) of the Southern Song Dynasty (1133-1279), in his annotations to his poem, said, "Zhang Yuanxiao is often seen with a catapult under his arm. He shoots iron pellets to dispel misfortunes and epidemics that plague people." So it was ridiculous to honour Zhang Yuanxiao as a son-bestower, as he was but an anti-epidemic god.

By the Ming and Qing dynasties, Taoist priests knowing the relationship between Meng Chang and Madame Huarui, changed the male image of Zhang Xian into the female image of Madame Huarui. From then on, the Son-Bestower in many counties and prefectures was represented as a woman. Colour paintings of unicorns bestowing sons or of King Wen with his hundred sons appeared on the walls of many temples. During the Lunar New Year and other holidays clay boy figurines were placed on the sacrificial tables or beside the Son-Bestowing Goddess for people to worship, with Taoist priests specially attending to collection of donations. Many temples had clay figurines for sale to the worshippers, one clay figurine costing a hundred coins to signify "Living to a hundred years." If one who bought a clay figurine then had a son born to him/her, he/she would have to make a large donation and give alms to the priests. The clay figurines would then be dressed in colourful costumes and sent to the temples to the beating of drums and gongs. This was called "Getting one son and paying back ten sons." If one had made a vow to the Son-Bestower and did get a son, he would have to redeem his vow to the Son-Bestower at the Lantern Festival (on the fifteenth day of the first lunar month).

CITY GODS

𝒯he City God was considered a basic-level god of the nether world in the old society and only people who had done good deeds in their lifetime could qualify as a City God after their death. According to *Strange Tales from Make-Do Studio* written by the Qing Dynasty writer Pu Songling (1640-1715), one had to pass an examination before becoming a City God. As feudal politics was getting more and more corrupt, by the end of the Qing Dynasty people in Guangzhou donated money to become a City God after death.

The following tales explain the origin of the City God and how he was granted honorific titles by the ruling house.

Commemorative City God

According to Chinese mythology, a City God is a guardian deity of a city. A Taoist classic says that the City God is a deity protecting a state against villainous characters and evil spirits. He could, at people's requests, bring rain when there was a drought and

City God

sunshine when there was too much rainfall, ensuring a good harvest for the people. Taoist believers regarded the City God as a deity having control over the dead. When Taoist priests offered sacrifices to "release the souls of the dead from the purgatory," they would send a note to the City God for permission to bring the souls to the altar.

In the Tang Dynasty and after, some enlightened officials emerged from among the numerous corrupt officials. People would honour these officials as "a parent of the people," or "a protective screen of the neighbourhood." After they died, the local people would honour them as a City God, in the hope that they could continue to offer protection. That is the reason why after the Tang Dynasty in many counties and prefectures sacrifices were offered to the City Gods and funeral eulogies were written in their honour. By the Song Dynasty, such sacrifices came into vogue throughout China. Many honest officials became City Gods after their death, such as Chun Shenjun in Suzhou, Wen Tianxiang in Hangzhou, and Qin Yubo in Shanghai.

Studies show that a number of the City Gods were truly good officials. For example, the City God of Guilin, Su Jian, was a local official in the Song Dynasty. He fought at the head of his soldiers against the invasion of *Jiaozhi* (ancient Chinese name for Viet Nam) and, running out of food and without reinforcements, he killed his family members first before killing himself. Legend had it that later, when *Jiaozhi* invaded Guilin again, the invaders saw Su Jian leading his soldiers northward. "City God Su has come to take his revenge!" they cried and fled in panic. After that, the people of Guilin established a Su Jian Temple and worshipped him as the City God. The City God of Hangzhou was Zhou Xin, Ming Dynasty provincial judge in Zhejiang. According to historical records, he was known for his honesty in government administration and for his firmness in cracking down on villainous characters and redressing injustice. His outspokenness offended the emperor and he was put to death. The commoners thus worshipped him as the City God. Some City Gods were bad characters deliberately supported by people with ulterior motives, while some were historical figures with no local connections.

City Gods with Honorific Titles Granted by Emperors

Granting honorific titles on City Gods began in 934, when Li Chongke, the last emperor of the Later Tang Dynasty, bestowed a princely title on a City God. Examples of emperors appointing a person as City God were many. For instance, Yuan Dynasty Emperor Wenzong (1329-1331) appointed the consort of a prince the City God of Beijing, although the local people worshipped Southern Song Dynasty national hero Wen Tianxiang (1236-1283) as Beijing's City God. Many cities made Northern Song statesman Fan Zhongyan (989-1052) their City God. Zhu Yuanzhang, or Emperor Taizu of the Ming Dynasty, took great interest in City Gods. Shortly after he became emperor, he had a splendid temple built for the City God at the national capital Nanjing. In 1369, believing that City Gods deserved a more illustrious position, he ordered the Board of Rites to conduct some investigations on the canonization of City Gods and report to him the results of their investigations. After hearing the report of the Board of Rites, Zhu Yuanzhang felt that sacrifices to City Gods had not been solemn enough and their official rank and position were not clear either. Then based on the hierarchy of Ming local officials, he laid down the honorific titles for City Gods and made them known to the public. He also prescribed the robes and headgear for City Gods at all levels and directed that each City God should lead some ferocious judges and yamen runners with bamboo rods and handcuffs in their hands. Thus City God Temples became like terror-striking yamens. Taoist priests in the pay of the ruling houses took the opportunity to fabricate a set of "theories' claiming that City Gods had the right to arrest people and send them to the nether world and the dead should be taken to a City God Temple to be tried. Zhu Yuanzhang also stipulated that before a new official took his post in the yamen, he had to take a bath and fast and offer sacrifices to the City God. In addition, he had to offer sacrifices to the god on the first and fifteenth day of each lunar month.

Zhu Yuanzhang showed keen interest in City Gods and bestowed titles on them, because he wanted to show off the authority of the Son of Heaven, and also because he believed that by so doing he could use the gods to help maintain his rule. He appropriated large funds from the state treasury to rebuild the City God Temple in the capital. Upon completion of the project, he said, "I set up the City God Temple in order that people would have something to fear and thus behave themselves." This ulterior motive of Zhu Yuanzhang's was also revealed in an imperial edict issued by his son Zhu Di, or Emperor Chengzu. This edict, inscribed on a stone tablet in the City God Temple in Beijing, then the national capital of the Ming regime, says he set up the temple in order to keep tabs on people's conduct and give them punishments or blessings on the merit of each case. Both Zhu Yuanzhang and Zhu Di hoped that, in this way, they could even detect people's secret activities and thus bring them under control.

Buying City Gods

In the thirty-second year of the Qing Dynasty Emperor Guangxu's reign (1906), when the money-crazy Zhang Tianxu, the so-called Heavenly Teacher of the sixtieth generation, saw that even official positions in the Qing Empire could be bought, he hit upon an idea of making a fortune for himself. He sent a "special envoy" to Sanyuan Temple in Guangzhou, where the envoy asserted that the Jade Emperor would set up an altar and hold a ceremony lasting seven days and nights in Guangzhou to make sacrifices to the deities to drive away disasters and bring blessings to the people. He spent fifty taels of silver to buy a lot of incense, candles and funerary paper for the occasion. Several days later, Zhang Tianxu himself came to Sanyuan Temple to preside over the ceremony in person. This news attracted large numbers of pious men and women worshippers to the temple.

On the third day of the ceremony, some of these worshippers, taking their cue from the "Heavenly Teacher," ran around alleging that there were 81,000 vacant City God posts in Heaven and that one who wished to fill one such post after his death should pay one hundred strings of cash before the "Heavenly Teacher" would recommend him for the post. Many people were taken in by the nonsense and offered their money generously to Zhang Tianxu. But as supply outstripped demand, at the end of the ceremony there were still three hundred vacant posts left unfilled. As the last resort, the "Heavenly Teacher" had to put them up to auction at the sale price of five strings of cash apiece.

LORD GUAN—
THE DEMON-SUBDUER

*I*n the feudal society of China, Guan Yu, a renowned general of the State of Shu in the Three Kingdoms Period (220-280), was honoured as the "Left Jade Emperor," "Military Sage," and "Great Demon-Subduing Emperor." He was respected as the supreme sage or deity and placed on a par with the Jade Emperor in Heaven. His statues were found in temples, on bridges or in pavilions as a guardian god. He was often portrayed in paintings sitting in a chair with a long beard and a stern and awesome expression on his red face. Standing behind him were Generals Zhou Cang and Guan Ping. Held in his hand was always his favourite long-handled, double-edged broadsword. People offered sacrifices and kowtowed to him when swearing to brotherhood, slaughtering an ox, praying for rain or sunshine, going to war, riding a horse, travelling by boat, seeking fortunes, exorcizing evil spirits, or praying for the birth of a son. Even before staging an opera, the actors would pay homage to him. The opera routines about Guan Yu required special singing patterns, costumes and other props and the actor who played Guan's role had to fast, kowtow to his picture and wear a small bronze statue of Guan Yu on his chest before appearing before the footlights.

From General to "Sage Emperor"

Guan Yu was a real historical figure and the number one of the five prominent generals under Liu Bei (161-223), founder of the state of Shu during the Three Kingdoms Period of the Eastern Han Dynasty (25-220).

Guan Yu, also known as Changsheng and Yunchang, was popularly called Lord Guan by later generations. He looked solemn and awesome with an imposing figure and a long beard. He was a native of Jiezhou (now Yuncheng County) in Shanxi. Some records say he was originally an ironsmith, while others say he was a bean curd pedlar. He was noted for his unusual strength, command of the martial arts and readiness to champion the cause of the underdog. Once a local despot filled up the only communal drinking well with stones and mud, so that the local people had to buy water at an exorbitant price from his well. An angry Guan Yu killed the despot and fled to Tongguan in Shaanxi. Together with Zhang Fei he went to Liu Bei for shelter and the three held a ceremony swearing to brotherhood at Peach Garden. The period in which they lived was a period of upheaval, when warlords fought with each other for supremacy in the scramble for power. Liu Bei was a man with high aims. He cherished the ambition to win the state power in the internecine strife.

Guan Yu followed Liu Bei faithfully. He fought many fierce battles for the latter's cause, winning the admiration of Cao Cao (155-220), founder of the State of Wei and a great poet and statesman during the Three Kingdoms Period.

Guan Yu was a man of integrity but he lacked farsightedness. Finally he was defeated and killed by the troops of the State of Wu. To appease the Wei, the Wu field commander had Guan Yu's head chopped off and sent to the Wei. The highest position Guan Yu held during his lifetime was Frontline General and the highest noble title he received from Cao Cao was Marquis of Shouting of the Han Dynasty. The *Eulogy to Later Han Ministers and Generals*, written by Yang Xi, a contemporary of Guan Yu, says, "Guan Yu and Zhang Fei were both stouthearted warriors." Later, the *History of the Three Kingdoms*, written by Chen Shou, who lived a little later than Guan Yu, says that Guan Yu was a right hand man of Liu Bei and that both he and Zhang Fei were brave soldiers "for whom ten thousand brave warriors were no match." So from the Western Jin Dynasty (281-318) to the Song Dynasty, people had regarded Guan Yu as a general of unusual valour.

Many people in the old days were superstitious.

Out of respect for heroic characters, they often made a cult of them as divine beings and built temples in their memory. Worship of Guan Yu as a god began in the Sui Dynasty. In *Records About Sakyamuni Buddha*, it is said that in the twelfth year of the Kaihuang reign of the Sui Dynasty (A.D. 592), when a monk named Zhi Ji of Tiantai Mountain went to Dangyang County to prepare the building of a temple for spreading Buddhism, he dreamed of a long-bearded deity, who claimed to be the Han general Guan Yu and master of Dangyang Mountain and wished to be converted to Buddhism to defend the laws of the religion. When Zhi Ji told the Prince of Jin his dream, the latter granted Guan Yu the title of Guardian God. Later generations, in light of the legend, listed Guan Yu as one of the Guardian Gods of Buddhism. Some temples, such as the Lingyin in Hangzhou, erected a statue of Guan Yu by the side of the Eighteen Guardian Gods of Buddhism. From then on, with the propagation of monks, Taoist priests and emperors, legends about Guan Yu as a god kept increasing. Building of the first Guan Yu Temple started in the Liang (502-557) or Chen (557-589) Dynasty during the Southern and Northern Dynasties Period in Dangyang County in Hubei, where Guan Yu met his death. By the Song Dynasty, Guan Yu Temples mushroomed throughout China, and more and more honorific titles and noble ranks were granted to him by emperors of various dynasties. Emperor Zhenzong of the Northern Song Dynasty officially granted Guan Yu the title "Outstanding King" and had it inscribed on a horizontal board and hung up in the Yuquan Temple of Dangyang County, to be followed by a long list of other titles by Emperor Huizong (r. 1101-1125) of the same dynasty, Emperor Gaozong (r. 1127-1162) and Emperor Xiaozong (r. 1163-1189) of the Southern Song Dynasty, and Emperor Wenzong (r. 1328-1329) of the Yuan Dynasty. By the Ming Dynasty, Emperor Taizu, thinking that there had been far too many titles heaped upon Guan Yu, abolished them all, keeping only his first title, the Marquis of Shouting.

During Ming Emperor Shenzong's Wanli reign period (1573-1618), a legend had it that "when a court envoy stopped over at a poststage in Luoyang, he dreamed of Guan Yu, who asked that a new house be built for him. The following day, when the envoy paid a visit to Guan Yu's tomb, he saw Guan Yu standing dimly in the white clouds. Then he offered a memorial to the emperor, suggesting to grant Guan Yu the title 'Miraculous Demon-Subduing Sage Emperor Guan. The emperor approved the proposal and sent a special envoy to offer sacrifices at Guan Yu's tomb and built a special temple in his memory."

The Qing Dynasty emperors also bestowed titles on Guan Yu. One, granted by Emperor Shunzhi (r. 1644-1661), ran as many as twenty-six Chinese characters. Emperor Yongzheng (r. 1723-1735) even bestowed the title of duke on Guan's great-grandfather, grandfather and father. Emperor Qian-long (r. 1736-1795) changed Guan Yu's posthumous title from "Heroic Lord" to "Lord of Loyalty and Justice." Emperor Xianfeng (r. 1851-1862) went a step further, bestowing a princely title on Guan's great-grandfather, grandfather and father. In 1914, the warlord government ordered that in sacrificial offering Guan Yu should be placed on the same footing as Yue Fei (1103-1142), a famous general and national hero of the Southern Song Dynasty.

The feudal rulers glorified Guan Yu as an embodiment of loyalty and justice in order to spread their feudal ethics and bind the people hand and foot, ideologically, so that they would not rebel against feudal oppression. To this end, rulers of various dynasties spread no end of lies about Guan Yu. For instance, in 1363, when the several-hundred-thousand-strong army of the peasant rebel leader Chen Youliang was routed by Zhu Yuanzhang, Zhu's military counsellor said Chen had been defeated by Guan Yu leading a hundred-thousand-strong army of heavenly warriors. Guan Yu was said to have made his presence or power felt in the Qing Dynasty's victory over a peasant rebellion in Aksu, Xinjiang during the reign of Emperor Daoguang (1836-1850). In the Ming Dynasty, the achievements Commissioner Pan Jirun made in harnessing the treacherous Huai River were also attributed to Guan Yu.

KING OF HELL—
SOVEREIGN OF THE GHOST
WORLD

The Jade Emperor is the highest ruler of the divine world. The King of Hell is the supreme sovereign of the ghosts. The "King of Hell" is a free translation of the *Yamaraja* (literally "twin sovereigns" in Sanskrit), who is the lord of the nether world in ancient Indian mythology. Buddhism followed the Indian myth and called him devil king in charge of Hades. Legend has it that he had eighteen judges in control of the eighteen layers of hell. It is said that the King of Hell and his sister were both sovereigns of Hades, or "twin sovereigns," the brother administrating male ghosts and the sister female ghosts.

The King of Hell is a "native" not only of India but also of Egypt. After this bodhisattva was imported into China, the Taoists tailored him to their own needs and made him China's "King of Hell," although he was at first called "Emperor of Mt. Tai." (In ancient China Mt. Tai, or East Mountain, one of the five sacred mountains of Chinese Buddhism,

King of Hell—Sovereign of the Ghost World

was allegedly the venue of ghosts.)

The legend about Mt. Tai as the venue of ghosts has a long history. The "Biography of Wu Huan" in the *History of the Later Han Dynasty* says "The soul of a dead person invariably goes to Mt. Tai." Later, by false analogy, Taoists identified Mt. Tai with the King of Hell in Buddhism and created many myths in connection with the King of Hell. One says that the Emperor of Mt. Tai was the fifth generation great-great-grandson of Pan Gu, the creator of the universe in Chinese mythology. His mother, a fairy called Mi Lun, once dreamed of swallowing two suns and then gave birth to two boys, Jin Chan and Jin Hong, the latter being the Emperor of Mt. Tai. Thus the King of Hell got a Chinese background.

Why, then, was the King of Hell identified with the Emperor of Mt. Tai, and not of the four other sacred mountains—the West Mountain, South Mountain, North Mountain and Central Mountain? Because Mt. Tai, also known as Mt. Dai or Dai Zong (Mountain Above Mountains), is in the east. The ancient people took the east as the source of change of all things and so Mt. Tai was honoured as the "first of the five sacred mountains." When a new emperor ascended to the throne, he would first go to Mt. Tai to hold memorial ceremonies to express his gratitude for being appointed to govern the people below. It is said that before the Qin Dynasty, seventy-two sovereigns of the Xia, Shang and Zhou dynasties had made pilgrimages to Mt. Tai. Since Qin

Shi Huang (r. 221-210 B.C.) unified China and founded the Qin Dynasty, an even greater number of emperors had offered sacrifices there. They considered it important to make pilgrimages to Mt. Tai. Many titles had been conferred on Mt. Tai, including the "Equalling-Heaven King" conferred by Emperor Xuanzong (r. 712-755) of the Tang Dynasty, the "Wise, Benevolent, Equalling-Heaven Emperor of East Mountain" by Emperor Zhenzong (r. 998-1022) of the Song Dynasty, the "Benevolent, Equalling-Heaven, Great-Life Emperor of East Mountain," or "Emperor of Mt. Tai the East Mountain" for short, by Emperor Shizu (r. 1279-1311) of the Yuan Dynasty. According to historical records, "Lord Mt. Tai ruled over 5,900 deities, handled the affairs of life and death in the mundane world and commanded ghosts of every description. For this reason, East Mountain Temples were built throughout China and sacrifices offered there year-round. These temples were actually an epitome of the feudal regimes. For example, one such temple in Xinxiang, Henan Province, was erected in 939 and rebuilt during the Song, Jin, Yuan and Ming dynasties. In its main hall was a statue of the Equalling-Heaven Emperor Huang Fei-hu (a character in the Ming Dynasty novel *Romance of the Canonized Gods*) and his attendants. It is said that the temple contained a Hall of the King of Hell, two corridors with twelve yamens responsible for civil affairs, and offices of marshals and generals for handling military affairs. Before Liberation, at the birth anniversary of the Emperor of East Mountain (on the twenty-eighth day of the third lunar month), superstitious activities were held. Another example was the temple on Baishan Mountain in Puxian County, Shanxi Province. The buildings, also known as the "East Mountain Temple's Eighteen Sections of Hell," were all built underground in 1318. They consisted of fifteen caves, one above the other, three of them each having two layers, forming eighteen sections of hell. Each section had statues of the King of Hell of every description. The top section was where the emperors of the five sacred mountains were, containing a travelling lodge with the statues of Huang Feihu and his attendants. The next lower section contained the statues of the formidable Kings of Hell in ten halls, each with a ghostly trunk and a human face. The last section contained the statues of six underworld judges and various ghost-officials. The judges looked stern and solemn, the ghost-officials running about in attendance. These statues were as large as life and wore vivid expressions on their faces, presenting a picture of purgatory in Chinese mythology. Beside the various statues were over 120 ghosts being put to torture, such as climbing a hill of knives, groaning in a millstone, hugging a burning pillar, cutting out hearts and tongues, gouging out eyes, sawing off limbs, and being fried in a burning oil crucible.

In Sanskrit the purgatory is *Naraka*, namely "bitter world" in free translation, as opposed to paradise. It is one of the "six paths" one is supposed to traverse after death according to his behaviour (or reincarnation in Buddhism) in his lifetime. The "six paths" are hell, hunger, beast, human being, heavenly god and demon. According to Buddhism, if one has done evil deeds or violated feudal moral principles, he would be relegated to the eighteen-layer hell to suffer after his death.

According to Taoism, the so-called Hades was located in two places, one in the north and the other in the south. The one in the south is Fengdu City, also known as Pingdu Mountain, in Sichuan.

The ancient city of Fengdu, legend has it, has been enveloped in a ghostly atmosphere for at least 1,600 years, after Ge Hong of the Jin Dynasty wrote the book *Biographies of the Gods.* Based on folk tales, it tells about how Yin Changsheng of the Eastern Han Dynasty and Wang Fangping of the Three Kingdoms Period cultivated themselves on Pingdu Mountain to finally become immortal after undergoing rigorous ascetic discipline. It is said that the crucible in which Yin refined his elixir pills, and a temple dedicated to the two, have remained intact in Pingdu Mountain. When referring to the two persons, later generations often said "Yin Wang," which in Chinese means "King of the Nether World." This probably is how Fengdu City came to become a purgatory, a place where a dead person is said to have to check in. To fool the people, the feudal rulers had many towers, bridges and halls built, according to the design in Chinese legends about the Hades in Ming Mountain, northeast of Fengdu City. The place was filled with a ghastly, blood-curdling atmosphere.

Actually Fengdu City has no connection whatsoever with ghosts and the King of Hell. Historically it was a secondary capital of the state of Ba during the Eastern Zhou Dynasty (about 300 B.C.). During the second year of the Yongyuan reign of the Eastern Han Emperor Hedi (A.D. 90), it was set up as a county. Because of the scenic Pingdu Mountain (changed to Ming Mountain after the Song Dynasty) northeast of the county town, it was named Pingdu County. In 589, in the Sui Dynasty, it was renamed Fengdu County.

The other purgatory, in the north, is Luofeng Mountain. It is said to be as high as 1,300 kilometres up and down and studded with ghosts' living quarters.

There are several explanations for the "eighteen-layer hell." Some held that six roots of sensation —eye, ear, nose, tongue, body and mind, six worldly environments and six recognizations formed eighteen boundaries, namely eighteen-layer hell.

THE DRAGON AND THE DRAGON KINGS

Legend About the Dragon

According to historical records, in the primitive clan society five thousand years ago, each clan had a totem of its own worshipping some kind of animal, such as ox, horse, tiger, deer, or snake. Later a powerful clan annexed other clans and created out of these a most fierce beast called dragon.

Records in ancient Chinese books about the dragon are numerous. One says, "The dragon is at the head of the four supernatural creatures (dragon, tortoise, phoenix and fish). It can become small or large, short or long, ascends to heaven after the spring equinox (the fourth solar term) and dives into the water after the autumn equinox (the sixteenth solar term)." As the dragon was a divine creature, so another record says, legendary immortals and emperors always rode a dragon when travelling or during an inspection tour. Still another says, "A dragon with scales is called Jiao-dragon, one with wings is Ying-dragon, one with horns is Qiu-dragon, and one without horns is Chi-dragon." There were 185 Dragon Kings in the dragon world that could create wind and rain. The Dragon Kings of the Four Seas are the four Dragon Kings depicted in the classical novel *Journey to the West*. In another classical novel, *Three Kingdoms*, a passage in chapter twenty-one describing the dragon says: "A dragon can be large or small; a large dragon can soar to the clouds while a small dragon can disappear into the water...."

What is a dragon like? As depicted in the Nine Dragon Screen in Beijing's Beihai Park, it is 5 metres high, 27 metres long and 1.2 metres thick. The Chinese character for dragon can be found in the oracle-bone inscriptions unearthed from the Yin ruins in Henan. It has four forms—the original complex form and three simplified ones. Both its original complex and simplified forms look like a wriggling animal with horns, a big mouth and body veins. The book *Classic of Mountains and Rivers* describes it as having a snake-like body and a human face, living at the foot of Zhongshan Mountain. In *Shen Nong's Materia Medica*, a lizard is described as a stone dragon and a dead snake's outer skin as a dragon robe. It can thus be seen that the imaginary dragon was like a snake or a lizard.

The Origin of Dragon Worship

The dragon is a symbol of the Chinese nation. The modern poet and scholar Wen Yiduo (1899-1946) said that the dragon was a fabricated creature. The pictures of dragons people see today are all like what Wang Fu of the Han Dynasty depicted. He said: "A dragon has horns like a deer, a head like a camel, eyes like a ghost, a neck like a snake, a belly like a clam, scales like a carp, ears like an ox, palms like a tiger, and talons like an eagle."

In 1978, Chinese archeologists discovered a large site of Longshan Culture in the Taosi Temple in Xiangfen County, Shanxi Province. The excavations revealed several large tombs from which was found a large pottery plate. It has a flat bottom and a polished inner wall which is decorated, in red and white, with the motif of a coiled dragon. The dragon has a body like a snake, a square head with two ears, a big mouth and sharp teeth, without horns or claws. As the dragon is like a snake but not a real snake and also like a crocodile but not a real crocodile, archeologists believed that the imaginary dragon might have its prototype in either of the reptiles. The pottery plate dates back to the 25th-20th century B.C., so this dragon might, at that time, be said to be the first image of a dragon discovered by scientists.

However, according to recent archeological data, in 1971, a dark-green jade dragon was found in a village in Inner Mongolia, with a body over fifty centimetres long, a tail shaped like an inverted C, a long mouth, a high nose, large eyes, and a long mane draping its back. Discovered by some peasants while planting trees, it was identified as a relic of the

Hongshan Culture in the Neolithic Age of about five thousand years ago. Nevertheless, this discovery raised a new question about the origin of the dragon. The jade dragon's head was like that of a pig, so some people thought that its original form might be a pig. Pig raising was closely connected with the development of primitive agriculture, so for a time pigs were offered as sacrifices to deities in primitive society. The image of the jade dragon shows that dragon worship might have originated from pig worship in some places.

In his article "The Origin of Dragons in China" Chen Qinjian pointed out, "From the excavation of the funerary objects such as clam, dragon and tiger from the No. 45 tomb in the Xishuipo site of Henan's Puyang County in 1987, Chinese scientists found, for the first time, from real objects to prove that about six thousand years ago the primitive people had conjured up the image of dragon that could be compared to the dragon designs on the ornamental articles in the Ming and Qing Dynasty palaces." The fabricated dragon frolicking in the clouds and water finally broke through the mist to become the symbol of the Chinese nation.

The Origin of the Dragon King

People in primitive society had probably seen the bones or fossils of dinosaurs. They might also have seen some kind of giant reptiles such as lizard, snake and boa. These probably were the basis for legends about the dragon. The primitive people, of course, could not explain many phenomena in the natural world; so when they saw the sky was overcast threatening a rain and such reptiles crawling about in the mountain valleys, they connected this natural phenomenon with those animals and created all sorts of myths and legends about how clouds and rains were ordered by the dragon. They considered the dragon able to fly into the sky, so the legends about the Yellow Emperor riding to the heavens on a dragon were created. The great poet Qu Yuan (340-278 B.C.) once also imagined himself riding a dragon to the sky. A legend in Zuo Qiuming's *Commentary on the "Spring and Autumn Annals"* recorded a story about an ethnic group good at raising dragons and called Huanlong (Dragon-Raising People), or the ancestors of Emperor Yao. A passage in the *Taiping Miscellany* gives this description of the Dragon King's palace: "South of Dongting Mountain there is a cave over a hundred feet deep, and after walking over fifty *li* across it one comes to a Dragon King's palace. The seventh daughter of the Dragon King of the East Sea takes charge of the magic pearl of the Dragon King with the help of over a thousand small dragons." This was the first record about the Dragon King.

In primitive society the dragon, in most cases, served as a totem of an ethnic group. After the birth of class society, it became a symbol of lucky signs and emperors claimed to be a "real dragon," and their descendants "sons and grandsons of the dragon." Later the emperors monopolized it as their own mascot and spread the myths about a dragon appearing in this or that place. During drought the emperors would set up alters to pray to the Dragon Star for rain. The common people also imagined that only dragons could bring rain.

By the Six Dynasties Period, with the spread of Buddhism in China, the story about the Black Dragon King in Buddhism also began to circulate. The Taoists sided with the Buddhists, claiming that dragons could be summoned to create rain. By the Song Dynasty, Taoism flourished and Dragon King Temples were set up in many places, and the practice of praying to the Dragon King for rain became popular. When praying for rain, Taoists said there were the Dragon King of the Four Seas and the Dragon King of the Five Directions, etc. During the Song Dynasty people prayed for rain by collecting scores of lizards in a jar and reciting charms to invoke the appearance of the dragons.

In the reign of Ming Dynasty Emperor Chengzu (1403-1424) and after, the rulers bestowed more favours on the dragon than ever before, conferring on the dragon honorific titles such as Dragon King. In 1724, Emperor Yongzheng of the Qing Dynasty went a step further, officially appointing the Dragons of the Four Seas (East, West, South and North seas).

THE FIRE GOD AND THE RED EMPEROR

*F*ire God is the most popular of the Chinese deities. In old China, Fire God Temples or Lingguan Temples were found in cities and the countryside. On the birthday of the Fire God (the eighth day of the first lunar month) pious men and women in various places would offer sacrificial pigs and sheep to the god amidst the beating of drums and gongs. According to *A Comprehensive Survey of Beijing's Temples*, there were seventeen Fire God Temples in the city of Beijing. One temple on a street in Zhengzhou, Henan Province, attracts large crowds of worshippers every year.

Wang Lingguan—the Fire God

According to records, the Fire God worshipped in Beijing, Zhengzhou and some other places is named Wang Lingguan. Legend says that he had three eyes and was a guard at the palace of the Jade Emperor. Taoists say he was ranked first among the twenty-six generals in the Heavenly Palace. Some say he

The Fire God

was a celestial general in the "Fire House."

Even Taoists could not tell how Wang Lingguan came to be the Fire God. They only knew Wang was a necromancer of the Song Dynasty, who learned Taoist doctrines in childhood and claimed to be able to get fire in his hand and hold it in his mouth, then later spit it out. With "divine light" on his body, he could walk in the dark as if in broad daylight. To deceive the world and win fame for himself, he painted an eye in the centre of his forehead to make himself "distinct from ordinary people." After he died, so the legend goes, the Jade Emperor appointed him "Heavenly General of the Fire House" in charge of the fire both in Heaven and the mundane world.

During the Song Emperor Huizong's reign (1101-1125) a quack doctor in Sichuan named Sa Shoujian fled into the mountains to avoid punishment because his wrong prescriptions had killed three patients. He gave up his profession as a doctor and became a Taoist priest. With not much seniority as a Taoist priest, he became poor. Then he remembered the three-eyed Wang Lingguan who had died long ago. Then Sa Shoujian claimed himself as a disciple of Wang, travelling from place to place making his living by practising witchcraft. To raise his own status, he alleged that Wang Lingguan was a Fire God in Heaven and a Fire Starlord on earth. Wherever he went, Sa Shoujian set up an altar to invite the Fire God Wang Lingguan to give medical treatment to patients. As Sa himself had been a doctor, he did cure some patients of their ailments, who out of gratitude for the protection of the god, set up temples in honour of Wang Lingguan as a Fire God.

During the Ming Dynasty's Yongle reign (1403-1424), a Hangzhou Taoist, Zhou Side, also claimed to be a disciple of Wang Lingguan as he wandered about deceiving the people at Kaifeng and Xinxiang in Henan. Later he came to Beijing, where he won the favour of Emperor Chengzu. The emperor made use of Zhou and honoured Wang Lingguan with the title "True Sovereign of Broad Favour" and ordered a Heavenly General Temple built. In Xuanzong's reign (1426-1435), the emperor changed its name to "Fire Starlord Temple" and added a statue of Wang Lingguan with a red face, three eyes, long whiskers, an open mouth and long teeth, wearing a suit of armour and an iron rod. But five statues were found in some of the Lingguan Temples because Song Dynasty Taoist priests wrongly took the Chinese character 王 (Wang) for the character 五 (Five).

The Fire Administrator Zhu Rong, or the Red Emperor

In Chinese mythology Zhu Rong is said to be an ancient emperor called Chidi (Red Emperor), who was called Fire Official by later generations. According to *Records of the Historian*, Zhu Rong was a "fire official" in Emperor Kao's time. He was very skillful at administering fire, and because of this he became revered as the Fire God.

Zhu Rong was born at a time when man worshipped fire. According to historical records, Zhu Rong could not only preserve and utilize fire but he had also streamlined the method of getting fire. So people called him Chidi (Red Emperor) as a token of their gratitude to him.

Zhu Rong, whose original name was Li, was the son of a tribal chief. He was described as having an imposing stature, broad shoulders and a red face. He was exceedingly clever and hot-tempered. In remote antiquity when the primitive people ate captured animals raw, a man called Sui Ren taught people how to cook with fire obtained by drilling wood. At that time people knew little about how to preserve and use fire. With a special interest in fire Li already showed great ability to handle fire at the age of nineteen. He knew how to preserve fire and how to use it to cook, keep warm, provide light and drive off fierce beasts, mosquitoes and insects, thus winning for himself the respect of the people. Once his father took the whole clan on a long migratory journey. Seeing that it was inconvenient to take fire along on the trek, he took a sharp stone with him. One night he got a log and started to bore it with the stone. He could not get the fire but only smoke after working at it for six hours. Shaking with anger, he stood up and flung the stone at a rock producing some sparks. This gave him inspiration with which he devised a new method of getting fire. He collected some dry reed catkins and put them near two sharp stones. Then he knocked the stones against each other and the sparks splashed on the reed catkins. This was immediately followed by a heavy smoke. He blew into the sparks with his breath and they flared up into flame.

When the Yellow Emperor in the Central Plains learned of Li's great invention, he invited him to his domain and appointed him the Fire Administrator. The emperor also bestowed on him the name of Zhu Rong (Wishing People Warmth), saying: "I wish you will bring warmth to the people forever." After that, people began to call him Zhu Rong instead of Li.

A tribal chief named Chiyou in the south often invaded the Central Plains. The Yellow Emperor ordered Zhu Rong to lead an army to fight against Chiyou. Chiyou's eighty-one brothers were all able to spout heavy smoke from their mouths. Nevertheless, Zhu Rong had ordered his soldiers to take torches and incendiaries with them. So his soldiers let off fire wherever they went, sending Chiyou and his men fleeing southward. The Yellow Emperor riding on a chariot equipped with south-pointing devices chased after them across the Yellow and Yangtse rivers all the way to Lishan Mountain and finally Chiyou was defeated and killed. In recognition of Zhu Rong's meritorious service, the Yellow Emperor bestowed on him a handsome reward and appointed him to administer the fire of the whole country. Zhu Rong was ordered to live in Hengshan, or South Mountain (one of the five sacred mountains in Chinese Buddhism) in the south to keep watch on the southern frontier.

After the Yellow Emperor returned to the north, Zhu Rong took over all the affairs of the south. Living on the highest peak of Hengshan Mountain, he often made inspection tours. When he saw the people there ate raw things and lived in the dark at night, he taught them how to get fire for cooking and to get light with pine torches. His efforts won him great respect among the people. Each year after autumn harvest, the local people would come to see him in groups, saying, "Zhu Rong, we thank you for bringing us so many benefits. We would honour you as an emperor. As fire is red in colour, we would call you Red Emperor."

Legend has it that Zhu Rong lived to be a hundred years old. After his death, the people buried him on a peak in Hengshan and named it Red Emperor Peak. The highest peak where he had lived in his lifetime was called Zhu Rong Peak, on which an imposing Red Emperor Temple was erected. Every year after autumn harvest, the people flocked there to worship him. Many years later, the rulers of the various dynasties honoured him as the Fire God or Fire Starlord, and the Red Emperor Temples became Fire God Temples.

SUN SIMIAO—
KING OF MEDICINE

At the centre of the hall in the King of Medicine Temple is enshrined a seated statue of a kindly, red-faced old man, wearing a flattop headdress and red robe with wide sleeves and a coloured belt. Standing on both sides are two boy attendants, one with a medicine bowl and the other with a medicine packet, a white-foreheaded tiger crouching to the front left. This bearded old man, with an unsophisticated air, is Sun Simiao (581-682), celebrated for generations as the "king of medicine" who had saved many lives with his excellent medical skills.

A Folk Physician

Born to a peasant family in today's Yaoxian County, Shaanxi Province 1,400 years ago, Sun Simiao was a child prodigy. He started learning to read and write at seven. With a retentive memory, he could recite one thousand words a day. His poor health made him determine to learn the art of healing. By the time he was twenty, he became

孫思邈

Sun Simiao—King of Medicine

proficient not only in medicine, but in the theories of Lao Zi, Zhuang Zi and other schools of thought during the Spring and Autumn and the Warring States periods. Emperor Wendi (r. 580-604) of the Sui Dynasty invited him to serve as the "doctor of education," both an official in charge of educational administration and a teacher for the children of nobility and high-ranking ministers. He refused on the pretext of illness. The two successive emperors of the following Tang Dynasty, Taizong (r. 627-649) and Gaozong (r. 650-683), asked him to serve in the court. Again he refused on the same pretext. Distressed to see the broad masses of the people suffering from both poverty and sickness, he dicided not to seek fame and gain, nor to become an official. Instead, he would conceal his identity and devote his entire life to the study of medicine and the relief with medicine of people's sufferings and disease.

A "Miracle-Working Physician"

Once, on his way to Changan to practise medicine, Sun Simiao, with a medical kit over his shoulder, came upon four people carrying a coffin heading for a burial ground, and an old woman following behind and weeping in deep grief. At the same time he found fresh blood dropping from the crack of the coffin. After making inquiries, he learned from the old woman that her daughter had died of difficult labour for quite some time. A careful examination of the blood from the coffin told him that the lying-in woman was still alive. At his suggestion, the coffin was opened to reveal the expectant mother with a sallow face and pale lips. He felt her pulse and found that it was still present, though feeble. He hurried to apply an acupuncture needle at a selected point. Meanwhile, he poured medicine down her throat. The patient came round and gave birth to a healthy baby. Witnesses admired him as a miracle-working physician who could resurrect the dead, and save two lives with one insertion of the needle.

Serving the People

Sun decided to render service to poor commoners with his excellent medical skill. To those who had no money to see a doctor, Sun gave free treatment. He vacated his own room to put up the patients from far-away places, decocted medicinal herbs for them, treated them with the same care given to his own family. Despite the darkness at midnight or violent storms, he never refused to go out to see a patient in need of help.

A patient suffering from retention of urine came to Sun for help. "The bladder can't hold so much urine," he thought, "and it's too late to take medicine to relieve his symptoms. There must be something wrong with the urine-discharging opening." Coincidentally he found a boy of the neighbourhood blowing a green-onion leaf for fun. Inspired, he found one to be used as a tube. He heated it over the fire, cut the tip, and inserted it into the urethra. He made a vigorious blow and, in a few seconds, the urine ran out through the green-onion tube and the patient recovered. Sun was the first to invent the catheterization method. Nowadays, for catheterization, a metal or rubber tube is used instead of a green-onion leaf. However, the principle of catheterizing is the same.

Sun was also the first in the world to discover night blindness, which people of mountain areas regarded as a strange eye disease. The sufferer had normal eyesight during the daytime but when night fell he could see nothing at all in a dim light just like a sparrow. "Why are the rich people immune to such a disease?" he asked himself. Estimating that it had something to do with people's diet, he went to the patients' homes to make investigations. Then he came to know that night blindness sufferers all came from poor families who lacked sufficient food, especially meat and other grain. "What medicine can cure such a disease?" According to a medical book, he recalled, the liver had much to do with the eyes. Knowing that the Wutai mountain area abounded in birds, wild sheep and wild boars, he bought the livers of such animals from some hunters and distributed them gratis among the night blindness sufferers. After eating the livers for a certain length of time they recovered.

Sun found that rich people often contracted beriberi characterized by swelling of the body, aching muscles and feebleness. "Why do the poor people suffer from night blindness, while the rich suffer from beriberi?" Sun pondered. "Possibly this has something to do with the diet as well. It might be caused either by an excessive amount of something or lack of it." A comparison between the diets of the poor and the rich revealed that usually the rich ate polished rice, wheat flour, meat, fish and greasy food, while the poor ate vegetables and coarse grain. The disease must have been caused by taking too much meat or refined flour or rice. A careful analysis showed that a large quantity of husks and brans contained in the coarse grain were all taken away from the polished rice and flour—leading to the conclusion that the beriberi might be caused by lack of rice husks and wheat brans, or substances of this kind. He tried out using these as remedies, and within six months, several sufferers were cured as expected.

One of the major factors for his success was that he never relied entirely on established practices found in past medical books. He attached more importance to learning from life and exploring in practice. One day when a patient having a pain in the leg came to see him, he practised several needle insertions, according to the points listed in medical literature, but failed to relieve the symptoms. Suspecting that the 365 points discovered by his predecessors were insufficient, he tried to find some new ones by asking the patient whether he had a sensation of soreness when pressing a spot with his thumb. Many times the patient shook his head. Finally he located the right point when the sufferer cried, "*Ah shi*" (Oh, yes). Sun applied an insertion and the pain in the leg disappeared immediately. It was Sun's major invention that acupuncture should be administered at the point which gives reaction of soreness. Afterwards the points thus found were named "Ah Shi," which are still widely used today in clinical practice. Furthermore, Sun collected quite a number of extraordinary points outside the course of the channels, and introduced the finger-length measurement, a method of locating points by using the finger-length of the patient as a criterion—a great contribution to the development of acupuncture technique in China.

Works by a Centenarian

As a Chinese saying goes, "It has been rare for people to live to be seventy since ancient times." Sun Simiao, however, lived to be 102. In his late years he remained robust and energetic, and wrote his two monumental medical works, *Prescriptions for Emergencies Worth Their Weight in Gold* and its thirty-volume *Supplement*.

The *Prescriptions for Emergencies Worth Their Weight in Gold*, also known simply as *Prescriptions*, was praised by practitioners of succeeding generations as a medical encyclopedia on clinical practice. Concise and rich in content, it contains the knowledge of various medical theories and practices required for a doctor. The book, also in thirty volumes, deals with 5,300 prescriptions classified into 232 categories, the scale so large that it was rarely found among medical works prior to the Tang Dynasty. It breaks with the conventional practice that for medical and pharmacological problems one has to consult the *Yellow Emperor's Canon of Medicine* and *Shen Nong's Materia Medica*, respectively. It also puts forth many original ideas about gynecology and pediatrics. "After a baby is born," Sun said, "the bloody dirt must be cleaned from its mouth and tongue with a piece of cotton wrapped over a finger." He proposed a number of first-aid measures for babies who came to the world without a cry and remained in a state of suspended animation. These views set forth in the seventh century agree with modern scientific principles—a proof of Sun's great medical attainments.

On his hundredth birthday, Sun finished another medical work, the *Supplement*, which contains all remedies he had collected in the last thirty years. Both the *Prescriptions* and its *Supplement* epitomize the pharmacological achievements made before the seventh century, hence occupying an important place in China's medical treasure-house. His other works include *On Fitness* and *On Happiness and Longevity*.

Origin of the "King of Medicine"

In the King of Medicine Temple on Mt. Wutai Sun frequented to gather herbs, his statue was enshrined as the "King of Medicine." This surely should be looked upon as a superstitious practice. But, viewed from another angle, it also reflected the memory the people cherished of him. The statement, "A celebrity will become a deity after his death," can be found in ancient writings. People tended to worship those who had made great contributions as gods—such as the legendary figures who were believed to have discovered the way of making fire, building houses and cultivating the land.

Sun's home village was a well-known producer of medicinal herbs. As he had practised medicine all his life for the people, and had a deep love for labour, he often went to the mountains gathering herbs. Totally disregarding the hardships and mishaps he might encounter, he took the trips as a rare pleasure because he could be bathed in the sunlight under a blue sky, breathe the fresh air in the mountains and drink sweet spring water at the foot of a steep cliff. He believed he would be tempered and tested by great nature whenever he was braving the wind or rainstorms. Actually, it was mainly because he worked in the mountains all year round that he was able to become a man of medicine enjoying good health and a long life.

Sun made his herb-gathering trips to the mountains on foot. With a small pick in hand and a basket on the back, he climbed overhanging cliffs and trekked through all the famous mountains in the vicinity of his village. On his return, he would dry and process the herbs he gathered and sometimes he even tasted them and tested the effect by taking them himself. He grew a great variety of herbal plants in his own garden and carefully studied their properties. He listed in his books the seasons suitable for collecting 233 herbs, and the proper time to pick their flowers, stalks and fruit. He also listed 383 herbs most in use, which, he wrote, should be collected at all times.

It was exactly because of his outstanding contributions to Chinese pharmacology that people venerated him as *Yao Wang* (King of Medicine) and gave Mt. Wutai its other name—King of Medicine Mountain. In a pavilion beside the King of Medicine Temple stand eight stone tablets inscribed with part of the prescriptions in common use from his great medical work *Prescriptions*. Another stone tablet on the southern peak of the mountain bears inscriptions about Sun Simiao's life story. In addition, there are sites of historical interest such as Taixuan (Great Profundity) Cave, the Xiyao (Washing Medicinal Herbs) Pond, and

Shengxian (Celestial Being) Terrace—all valuable monuments in his memory. In 1961 the Ministry of Posts and Telecommunications issued a set of stamps to commemorate well-known scientists in ancient China, two of which were devoted to Sun Simiao.

Through the centuries, people revered him as the "King of Medicine," *zhenren* (immortal), "Retired Scholar" and "Great Physician for the Masses of the People." Emperor Huizong of the Song Dynasty awarded him a posthumous title Miaoying Zhenren (Prodigious Immortal). In many places temples were built to house his statues for people to worship. There are many more widely-spread stories about his admirable skill in curing diseases, some of which have been turned into fairy tales. The legend of the tiger to the front-left of his statue is no less fascinating.

When Sun lived as a hermit in the mountain, so the story goes, he often went out to make a house call with a donkey carrying the medical kit for him. Once, as he concentrated on examining a patient, the donkey slipped away to the mountaintop and was eaten by a tiger. Furious, he drew a charm to summon all the tigers in the area. "Who has eaten the donkey? Let it stay here, and the others may get away," he shouted. One tiger, as it turned out, crouched on the ground meekly waiting to be dealt with. Since then, the animal had taken the place of the donkey to carry the medical kit for Sun and became his inseparable companion.

LU BAN—
ANCESTOR OF ARTISANS

Lu Ban and His Family

Lu Ban, a real historical figure, was the finest building artisan in ancient China. According to ancient literature, in his time when the level of productive forces was not yet high, he had made outstanding contributions for his inventions of production tools and renovation of weapons, which won him high praise across the land. Over the past two thousand years he has been honoured and commemorated as the "Master Founder" by Chinese building artisans.

Lu Ban (c. 507-444 B.C.), also known as Gongshu Ban, lived in a time when the Warring States Period was replacing the Spring and Autumn Period, and when the slave system was changing over to the feudal system. The development of social production provided a material foundation for the disintegration of slavery and the rise of the feudal system. Slave uprisings and insurrections rose one after another. All this led to the breakthrough of the government-operated handicraft industry monopol-

Lu Ban—Ancestor of Artisans

ized by slave owners, and the emergence of independent individual handicrafts. It was quite possible that Lu Ban was an emancipated slave artisan of this period, who could travel from place to place working on his own.

Lu Ban came from several generations of artisans. His father was a veteran carpenter with forty years of experience. Since childhood Lu Ban was diligent and eager to learn. He often worked together with his father, doing odd jobs. At the age of ten, he was able to do all the ordinary handicraft work. The axe or chisel, whenever in his hand, moved very fast and rhythmically. He kept himself busy making small wooden tools. In this way, he had learned from his father many manual skills. He knew how to build a house or bridge, manufacture a machine, and carve.

When Lu worked at home, he often asked his mother to help by pulling at the other end of the line in the ink marker. This interfered with the mother's own work. One day when Lu was not around, she fastened a large wooden hook to the line so that the latter could be fixed at one end of a piece of wood—hence inventing the wooden hook with which one person was enough to print the guidelines. Today the iron hook has taken the place of the wooden one, but its name *ban mu* (Lu Ban's mother), as carpenters of later times called it in her memory, remains unchanged.

Lu Ban sometimes asked his wife to help stabilize

a woodblock he was planning. One day she suggested nailing a short stake on the bench to replace her hands. Lu Ban thought it a good idea and acted accordingly. To date, the wooden stake is still called ban qi (Lu Ban's wife).

According to historical records, many tools used by carpenters were invented by Lu Ban, such as the square (also known as Lu Ban square), plane, drill, ink marker, chisel and shovel. The appearance of these tools reduced strenuous labour and raised work efficiency and technological levels. Lu Ban was especially known for his super skill in woodwork.

A story says that Lu Ban made a wooden kite, which flapped its wings and flew into the sky. Overjoyed, he went to the thinker Mo Di, also known as Mo Zi, to show off his achievement. Mo said, "The thing you've made is not as good as my invention, the axle pin outside the wheel of a cart. I whittled a piece of wood three inches long into an axle pin which enables the cart to carry a freight weighing fifty *dan*.* You can be counted as ingenious only when the thing of your making is beneficial to the people. If not, you are to be counted only as stupid." Deeply impressed, Lu began to devote his energy and talent to the mastery of techniques for making tools beneficial to production and people's daily life.

---

* 1 *dan*=50 kilogrammes.

Lu Ban's Inventions

The carpenter's saw and plane were said to have been invented by Lu Ban. Once in preparation for building a palace, together with his apprentices, he went to Nanshan Mountain lumbering. Felling trees with an axe was tiring and maddeningly slow. The timber they had cut fell far short of demand. As the date for starting the construction was drawing near, Lu Ban was burning with impatience. One day, he went to a precipitous peak to select timber. All of a sudden his hand was badly scratched as he stripped a handful of blades from wild grass on the roadside. Greatly puzzled, he carefully examined the plant and found its blades with two edges of sharp teeth —which had cut his hand. Maybe, he thought, an iron blade with an indented edge could fell a tree more easily. He asked a blacksmith to forge several such blades, which, as expected, not only saved a lot of labour, but speeded up lumbering. Within a couple of days all the timber needed was ready. The blade with an indented edge was the predecessor of the saw in common use today.

Then another problem cropped up: How to make a piece of wood even and smooth? This could be achieved by scraping with a knife, but it would take too much time and effort. Hacking with an axe would make a round surface. On the principle of scraping with a knife and hacking with an axe, he made repeated experiments and finally invented the plane which greatly facilitated the processing of wood.

In addition, Lu Ban solved many problems people had come across in their daily lives. With the development of agriculture, they were required to husk grain and grind beans and wheat—an important but strenuous daily routine. The previous method was to pound rice, wheat or other food grains in a stone mortar with a wooden club or stone pestle. This took a lot of energy but with low efficiency, and the husked rice and flour thus produced were uneven in fineness. It was found later that grinding was more efficient than pounding. Inspired by the way the working people rubbed rice with their hands, so a legend goes, Lu Ban tried to grind grains first with two rough stones. Thee he made closely-cut shallow grooves in the surfaces of the pair of flat, circular stones, and fixed an axle in the centre (called mill umbilicus by people of later generations), hence creating the predecessor of the stone mill used by the Chinese people for more than two thousand years.

Another legend says that the lock was available long before. However, it was not ingeniously made and could be easily opened. After pondering over the matter for a long time, Lu Ban improved the old lock by hiding the gear inside. This provided the groundwork for modern locks.

Lu Ban also contributed a great deal to the amelioration of the chariot. He was believed to have transformed it into a mobile wooden horse-drawn vehicle. Enlightened by the legend, many people of later times had made studies and experiments. Viewed from today's angle, it was an exaggerated statement that the wooden horse-drawn chariot could run automatically and so fast that it soon vanished from sight. But it cannot be denied that Lu Ban's skill was really outstanding in his time.

Coming to the weapons, it was said that the scaling ladder for attacking a city and the *gouju*, a naval-battle weapon manufactured by Lu Ban, had played an important role in warfare. Following the advice of Mo Zi, he no longer made such tools, and turned to the inventions closely related to production and daily life for the benefit of the people.

Lu Ban did a lot in architecture and carving. According to historical records, the phoenix he carved on a rock was so lifelike that its feathers seemed dancing with the wind. On Mt. Baoshi in Luoyang, Henan Province, Lu carved a three-dimensional "map of China" out of a rock.

For thousands of years, stories about Lu Ban's inventions were told and retold among people generation after generation. To show their love and respect, carpenters, stone masons, bricklayers and even blacksmiths in some places worshipped him as "Master Lu Ban" or "Master Founder," crediting certain collective creations or unique inventions to him. Therefore, stories of his inventions are actually stories of inventions of the working people in ancient China. His name has become a symbol of their diligence and wisdom.

Lu Ban—Legendary Builder of Zhaozhou Bridge

By the Tang Dynasty, legends of Lu Ban had appeared in large numbers and spread through the country. The most popular was the one about "Master Lu Ban Building the Zhaozhou Bridge." The date when the legend began to appear remains unknown, but it was first recorded in the historical data of early Yuan.

There were two stone bridges in Zhaozhou, the legend says, one located in the south of the city, and the other in the west. The bigger one, in the south, was built by Lu Ban, while the smaller one, in the west, was built by Lu Jiang, Lu Ban's younger sister.

Lu Ban and his sister traveled from place to place. One day, when they arrived in Zhaozhou, the first thing they saw was the broad, deep Jiao River in their way. At a ferry crossing, there were crowds of people, yelling and shouting, trying to be the first to cross the river to go to town. The current was swift. The two ferryboats available carried only a few people each time. It would be noontime soon; some would-be passengers were there since the morning, still waiting to be ferried. They were complaining bitterly.

"Why don't you build a bridge over the river?" he asked the people.

"The Jiao River is ten-li wide," they chorused. "The water is deep and whirls the sand. We've greeted visitors from across the land, but no skilled craftsmen have ever been found." Lu nodded and, examining the flow of the water and the topography, he decided to build a bridge for the people of Zhaozhou.

Everywhere she went, Lu Jiang had often heard complimentary comments on her brother's skill and ability and had cherished the dream of outshining him some day. This time, she was determined to compete with her brother to see who was the better. She suggested that two bridges be built—one in the south, the other in the west. These would be built separately, Lu Ban and she each responsible for one bridge. The construction should be started at dusk and finished at dawn. The one who failed to complete the project as soon as the cock crowed would be the loser. Lu Ban was to build the bridge in the south, his sister would build the one in the west.

Lu Jiang came to the western part of the city, where she began to collect materials and worked in great haste. By midnight, she was putting the finished touches on the new bridge. Confident that she would be the winner, she secretly rushed to the southern part of the city to see how her brother was getting along with his project. To her surprise, she did not find a single trace of the bridge at the

99

designated site. Then she saw a man descending from the Taihang Mountains to the south, driving a large flock of sheep. When she came closer, she found the man was her brother. What he drove was not sheep, but snow-white, glossy stones. Her heart sank at the sight of these stones. How solid and beautiful the bridge would be if built with such fine material, she thought. Surely the bridge she had built would be no match for her brother's. She decided to do some extra work on her bridge, so she hurried back to her bridge and carved on the railings various designs depicting the Cowherd and the Weaving Maid, Eight Immortals Crossing the Sea, a phoenix worshipping the sun, a dancing dragon sporting with a phoenix, and countless exotic flowers and rare grasses. Proud of her carving, she went to see her brother. Now his bridge was near completion, with only two stones waiting to be laid at the end. At the crucial moment, she began to crow like a cock at the top of her voice, which caused all the cocks around the village to do the same. On hearing this, Lu Ban hurried to place the two stones properly to finish the construction on schedule.

Thus two solid, handsome bridges were built overnight at Zhaozhou. The next day the news caused a sensation among people in neighbouring prefectures and counties. Word also came to the Eight Immortals living on a fairy isle. Zhang Guolao, the meddlesome immortal, led his white donkey out of the shed. In the left end of a long bag on its back, he put the sun, and in the right he put the moon. He asked King Chai to push a one-wheel barrow carrying the four famous mountains to go with him to Zhaozhou. On their arrival at the bridge, Zhang asked loudly, "Who is the builder of the bridge?"

"It's me," Lu Ban answered. "What's the problem?"

Pointing his finger at the donkey and barrow, Zhang asked, "If we pass the bridge, could it bear the weight?"

Lu Ban laughed. "Large flocks of big mules and horses have passed over it, let alone a donkey and a barrow. Don't worry, just go ahead."

Zhang and King Chai smiled and continued their trip. As soon as they stepped onto the bridge, it began to sway and was on the brink of collapse. Lu Ban rushed under the bridge to support it. The incident did not bring any damage to its body or foundation. Instead, it became more solid than before. Only the southern end of the bridge deviated to the west about several metres. Today, on the bridge there are still eight donkey hoofprints left by Zhang Guolao's animal, and a one-metre-long rut made by the barrow pushed by King Chai. On the underside of the bridge, impressions of Lu's two hands can still be seen. A New Year print deals with Master Lu Ban supporting the bridge with his hands.

After crossing the bridge, Zhang Guolao looked back at Lu Ban, and remarked sarcastically, "I really feel sorry for your eyes!" Lu Ban, deeply ashamed of his failing to recognize the worth of the donkey driver, gouged out one of his eyes with his hand, put it on one side of the bridge and left quietly. It was picked up later by Horse God, who stuck it to his own forehead. This explains why carpenters of later times always use one eye when using a plumb-line, and why the statue of the Horse God had three eyes.

Since Tang and Song times, the guild system was widely adopted, and many crafts had their own guilds, which by the Ming-Qing period had changed to trade associations. Each trade had its own master founder or trade god. Lu Ban was the trade god of carpenters, stone masons and bricklayers. In early Ming, temples were built to worship Lu Ban in Beijing and other places. The date for offering sacrifices also varied in different localities.

Lu Ban, though worshipped as god, is entirely different from the deities created by the people. "Master Lu Ban," as described in the book *Gods of Ancient China*, "is an outstanding representative of Chinese skilful craftsmen, an embodiment of the wisdom and creative power of the working people.... He was a kindly, honest elder, who, wearing shabby clothes, was busy helping people of his trade in trouble." Today, "Show off one's proficiency with the axe before Lu Ban" remains a common phrase in describing a person who tries to display his slight skill before an expert. Furthermore, people usually call some of the outstanding craftsmen as "Living Lu

Ban" or "Young Lu Ban"—a distinguished honour given to this "ancestor of artisans."

GODDESS OF HEAVEN— GODDESS OF THE SOUTH CHINA SEA

Tianhou or Tianfei (Goddess of Heaven) was also known as the "Goddess of Mazu." Tianhou Palaces (also called Mazu Palace or Mazu Temple) are found in Fujian, Taiwan and Shanghai.

Around Tianjin, however, Tianhou was called Niang Niang (Goddess), and the Tianhou Palace was named Niang Niang Temple. Those with superstitious ideas held that the Goddess had great prestige and supernatural power. They believed that the poor could pray to her for prosperity, the childless for the birth of a son, the sick for happiness and avoidance of trouble, and those in difficulty for protection.

There were many legends about the Goddess. Some held that she was the mother of the Jade Emperor in Heaven; some regarded her as the sister of Queen Mother of the West. But it was widely agreed that she was a kind, gentle grey-haired old lady. Hence when praying to her, the worshippers usually called her Old Goddess. Actually most of the legends maintained that she was not a deity, but a human being; not an old lady, but a young girl who lived between 960-987. According to the book *Gods of Ancient China*, the Goddess of Heaven was a real person, whose original name was Lin Mo, a native of Putian, Fujian Province. Coming from a fisherman's family, she was a bright, pretty girl and loved to help people in adversity. She was a good swimmer and had gone fishing on the sea with her elder brother since childhood. Facing howling winds and braving vicious billows, she often rowed a boat to rescue people in distress at the risk of her life. Her heroic deeds gained attention far and wide earning for her the loving name "Goddess."

On a stormy day more than ten centuries ago, she came to the aid of an overturned merchant ship. She rescued nine of the ten people aboard; the one left was tossed a great distance away by a huge wave. Disregarding her own safety, she swam to catch him. He was saved from drowning, but Lin Mo, exhausted, drowned in the rolling billows.

Reluctant to admit that she had died in an accident, people preferred to think that she had become a goddess. According to legend, "Music resounded in the air and a crimson cloud looking like a carriage was descending from the heavens. The Goddess got on it and soared to the sky." The legend adds: "Somebody saw the Goddess in red garment flying over the sea." The people of Putian, her hometown, built a temple in her memory.

After her death, the Goddess was said to have become more miraculous. Once, a violent windstorm was raging over the sea and overturned a dozen fishing boats. All the fishermen fell into the water. At the critical moment, the Goddess was seen coming. With a fish fork, she set the overturned boats right one by one and pulled the fishermen on to the boats from the water. In a moment the wind subsided and the waves calmed down, and all people in distress were saved.

On another occasion, smallpox spread around the area and many children fell seriously ill. Their parents went to all temples they could find to burn incense and give pledges before deities, but in vain. One night, they dreamt of the Goddess bringing medicine for their children. The following day, all the young patients recovered. So every family burned incense to show its gratitude.

Afterwards, businessmen who often put out to sea donated funds to build a temple for the Goddess. Pilgrims came in increasing numbers to pray for happiness or redeem a vow. Some brought an embroidered silk garment and draped it over the shoulders of the statue; some made a soft horizontal board with velvet and hung it on the wall of the shrine-hall. Inscriptions on such boards read: "Blessing and Protecting Our Newly-Born Baby," "Protecting the People," "Blessing and Protecting Our Locality," and "Known for Power on the Sea." The story of the Goddess' invincible might spread through the entire province of Fujian and the coastal areas south of the Yangtze River.

Marine transportation had developed greatly since the Yuan Dynasty. More and more people from Fujian and Guangdong came to the north with ships loaded with large quantities of grain and merchandise. They also brought stories of the Goddess' supernatural power, which, seasoned with extravagant details when told and retold, became increasingly magical. Merchants traveling by sea contributed money to build temples for the Goddess in Dagu and Tanggu along the coast and places along the Haihe River. Some even attracted several tens of thousands of pilgrims each year, not only from the neighbouring counties, but also Hebei, Shandong and provinces in the northeast.

Emperors of various dynasties glamourized the Goddess. During a period of eight hundred years, on forty occasions they granted her titles which, when put together, ran to sixty characters, including "State-Protecting Sage," "Protector of the State and the People," and "Prodigious Goddess." Lin Mo's status was promoted from Miss, Lady, Saintly Goddess to Goddess of Heaven. At first, sacrifices were offered only by commoners. As time went by, sacrificial rites were held by high officials sent by the court, and went on the record. Despite this, people continued to call her Niang Niang and her temple Niang Niang Temple.

The Tianhou Palace outside the east gate of Tianjin was built in 1326 during the Yuan Dynasty with funds donated by rich maritime merchants. Tradition claims that a big antique trader from Guangdong travelled by ship with goods valued at ten thousand taels of gold. On its way to the north, a windstorm blew up and snapped off the mast. A huge wave crashed through the hold, threatening to overturn the ship. The merchant prayed to Heaven for safety, pledging to build a temple if he could survive. At this point a bright light suddenly appeared. He saw a neatly dressed goddess standing at the prow. She waved her arms to the sky and the storm subsided at once. Then the Goddess disappeared. Pleasantly surprised, the merchant thought, "It must be Niang Niang who has saved my life."

The rich merchant arrived at Tianjin safely. To express his thanks, he donated part of his property to build a temple for the goddess. Other merchants followed suit. Bricklayers, carpenters and painters involved in the project charged only half price for their services. Within a year, the magnificent temple was completed.

Tradition claims that her birthday fell on the twenty-third day of the third lunar month. Since early Qing, every year on that day, a religious festival was held to greet the Goddess with several dozen groups of folk artists participating. Performances including magic drum, lion dance, flower drum and pole tricks were given in the street, presenting a scene of bustle and excitement. The

Goddess would be taken in an "imperial carriage" from her palace and escorted by the artists, who were performing all the way to her "parents home" in the Fujian-Guangdong Guild Hall in the northern part of the city. She would stay there for three days and then be escorted back to the palace by the same performing artists. As the festival was specially held for the Goddess, it was also called Niang Niang Festival.

One day the Qing emperor Qianlong came to Tianjin on the birthday of the Goddess. He watched the performances with great admiration, and awarded the festival organizers several yellow mandarin jackets and festival banners. The organizers looked upon this as the highest favour they had ever received. After that, the Niang Niang Festival was renamed "Imperial Festival."

Cui Xu, a poet of the Qing Dynasty, wrote this poem describing the lively atmosphere when the Goddess was being greeted:

Teams are moving about, each urged to perform their own.
Like spring thunder, playing, singing and cymbal-drum beating resound.
Countless spectators jostle each other in lanes and streets,
Just to welcome the Goddess' arrival amid a myriad of bright lamps.

When the religious festival was celebrated in the Ruyi Nunnery in the twentieth year of Qing Emperor Guang Xu's reign, smoke curled up from burning joss sticks which ignited the altar curtain causing a big fire. Devout worshippers scrambled to flee for their lives. Believing that there was a precious pearl in the Goddess' head, someone stole the head in the confusion. Panic-stricken, the county magistrate and the festival organizers sent bailiffs to pursue and capture the offender, and no clues were found. Then a high price was offered for the capture, but still in vain. Finally a head of *nanmu* wood was fixed on the statue. Soon after, the allied forces of the eight powers invaded Tianjin in 1900. Since then the celebrations of the Imperial Festival had to be stopped.

It was said in the past that fishermen or navigators all knew the Goddess of Heaven, and paid religious homage to her.

It should be pointed out that the Goddess' reputation was closely associated with conditions under which navigation was conducted. In those days, navigating on the sea was hazardous. With the treacherous and changeable weather, safety could not be guaranteed. At a time when the imperial court attempted to reassure the public, and the people wanted to find a protecting deity on the sea, naturally the Goddess of Heaven was the best choice. Hence, Tianfei Palaces were built in many coastal cities and towns. Later on, the Goddess of Heaven travelled across the sea to Southeast Asia to be worshipped there.

TAOIST MASTER ZHANG— FOOD-EATING IMMORTAL

Master Zhang, the Five Pecks of Rice Sect, and the Zheng Yi Sect

Master Zhang, whose full name was Zhang Ling, or Zhang Daoling (34-156), was the founder of the Five Pecks of Rice Sect of Taoism during the Eastern Han Dynasty. A native of what has now become Fengxian County, Jiangsu Province, he studied in the Imperial College and had knowledge of the Five Classics*. During the reign of Emperor Mingdi (r. 57-75) he served as prefect of Jiangzhou Prefecture (today's Chongqing), and practised meditation in Heming Mountain in today's Dayi County, Sichuan Province in the reign of Emperor Shundi (r. 125-144). In 141, he wrote twenty-four Taoist texts and institutionalized Taoism, which was also called the Five Pecks of Rice Sect, Rice Sect, or Spirit Sect, calling himself Occult Master of Great Purity. Its believers had to pay five pecks

---

*The Book of Songs, The Book of History, The Book of Changes, The Books of Rites and The Spring and Autumn Annals.

Taoist Master Zhang—Food-Eating Immortal

of rice as contribution to support the church. It emphasized repenting one's mistakes and believing in Taoist canons. It propagated its doctrine by praying and drawing charms, and gave treatment with magic water or incantations.

Zhang divided his followers into twenty-four *zhi* or sections, and appointed *jijiu* to lead them. He was later honoured as Taoist Master (some say that the title was given by himself). Taoism worshipped Lao Dan (Lao Zi), the pre-Qin philosopher, as its founder, deified him as the supreme celestial god and named him Lord Lao Zi, with the five-thousand-character *Dao De Jing* (*The Way and Its Virtue*) as its basic book. In fact, this is a far-fetched analogy, as Lao Zi had nothing to do with the Taoist religion. The new converts were called *guizu* (devil soldiers) and the core ones were called *jijiu* (leaders). *Zhi* was set up as the unit for preaching purposes. It was said that in A.D. 143, during the Eastern Han Dynasty, there were altogether twenty-four *zhi*, most of them in what is now Sichuan Province. After the death of Zhang Ling, his son Zhang Heng, also known as Zhang Lingzhen, took over his mantle as "Master Successor." According to legend, Zhang Heng "went up to Heaven in daytime" in 179. After he died, his son Zhang Lu continued preaching the Taoist religious doctrine.

In 191, during the regin of Emperor Xian Di, Zhang Lu, then a military officer under Liu Yan, prefect of Yizhou, led his men in defeating Su Gu, prefect of Hanzhong, and seized that area. After the death of Liu Yan, his son Liu Zhang succeeded to his position. Learning that Zhang Lu refused to obey orders, Liu killed all his family members in Sichuan, including his mother and wife. This drove Zhang to set up at Hanzhong a separatist regime integrated with Master Zhang's religion. Actually it was a small religious state in an area nestled in the mountains.

Here in this state official ranks of the Han court such as prefect and magistrate were replaced by work titles adopted by the Five Pecks of Rice Sect. Ordinary followers were called *guizu* or devil soldiers, officials called *jijiu*, and high officials called *zhitouda jijiu*. Zhang Lu styled himself *shijun* (Master Sovereign). These titles, though with pronounced religious colour, were free from bureaucratic airs. According to their regulations, those who fell ill should confess their mistakes to a god and pray for protection from disaster. *Jijiu* were assigned to administer local political affairs. On all roads were erected "charity houses" where travellers could put up for the night free of charge. In the charity house were stored "charity rice" and "charity meat" for travellers to eat, also free of charge. But, if anyone had taken more than he needed, it was said, he would be made a victim to a disaster by the divinity. In those days the tangled warfare among warlords produced large numbers of refugees, for whom the establishment of "charity houses" was really a good measure of the government.

Regarding penal codes, they laid stress on light and stayed punishment. Minor offenders were required to build a section of road only a hundred steps long. Offenders could be pardoned three times. Only when they refused to mend their ways, would they be punished by law. It was strictly forbidden to slaughter domestic animals and make and drink wine in spring and summer in a bid to protect agricultural production and guard against extravagance and waste. As such measures of Zhang Lu more or less met the needs of the people, he enjoyed the support, according to historical records, of the people of Han and minority nationalities in the area under his control. He reigned for nearly three decades and made Hanzhong the most tranquil place.

During his reign over the Hanzhong area, Zhang Lu did not thoroughly cut off contacts with the feudal imperial court. Only because the warlords in the Central Plains fought each other ceaselessly, was he able to exercise sovereignty over that part of the country under his control. In 215 Cao Cao, one of the warlords, launched an offensive on Hanzhong. Though temporarily hiding himself in Bazhong in Sichuan, Zhang Lu soon surrendered to Cao Cao, and was made a general and a marquis. Hence this "Master Sovereign" became a powerful marquis overnight. That is to say, from then on the Five Pecks of Rice Sect began to serve as a tool of the feudal ruling class, and the measures temporarily beneficial to the people also came to an end.

Zhang Lu died during the Western Jin period. His son Zhang Sheng became the Tianshi Dao's (Five Pecks of Rice Sect) Taoist Master of the fourth generation. Legend says that some time between 307 and 312 he moved to Longhu Mountain in Jiangxi Province. Honouring Zhang Ling as the head of the church and "Master Zheng Yi," he founded later the North-South Tianshi Dao. During the Tang-Song period, this sect gradually merged with other sects and evolved into the Zheng Yi Sect during the Yuan Dynasty. In a word, Taoist followers believed in the wish of the "god" expressed through divination. The magic charms, they thought, were the script of the "celestial god"; putting up prayers was the rite for making requests to the "god"; and secret incantations were the "god's" stern language. They practised divination to decide whether their luck was good or ill. They wrote magic charms to "chase away evil spirits"; they prayed to "avert a misfortune or disaster and to beg happiness." They chanted secret incantations to "avert a disaster and drive away evil spirits and fierce beasts."

After A.D. 312, Master Zhang of the fourth generation was said to have stepped into the stage of self-reflection and reform of creed from the initial stage—the founding of the religion. During this period, the Five Pecks of Rice Sect, which was subject to the reform by Kou Qianzhi, a priest from Songshan Mountain, according to the needs of the

Northern Wei Dynasty rulers, enjoyed the trust of the latter. The descendants of Zhang Daoling also made some changes on the religious doctrine, specifically advocating the ideas of "loyalty and filial piety" and "assisting the country and protecting the people." In Tang times, emperors Xianzong (r. 847-859) and Xizong (r. 874-888) granted titles of "Grand Tutor" and "Grand Master," respectively, to Zhang Daoling. During the Song period, beginning with Zhenzong (r. 998-1022), all emperors titled him "Xian Sheng" (the highest title for a Taoist priest in the Song Dynasty) of different descriptions. Emperor Huizong, a fatuous and self-indulgent ruler who styled himself Taoist Patriarch, dreamed of becoming an immortal. Many times he asked Zhang Jixian, Taoist Master of the thirtieth generation, about the way and the method of achieving longevity. He allocated fifty thousand pecks of rice to build a Taoist monastery of the Zheng Yi Sect on Longhu Mountain in Jiangxi Province. In the late Southern Song period, Emperor Lizong conferred the title of Miraculous Master on Zhang Ke, the Taoist Master of the thirty-fifth generation, and promoted the charms of the Longhu, Gezao and Maoshan mountains. The Master, on the one hand, accepted the title from the Southern Song emperor. On the other, he secretly transmitted Kublai Khan (the first emperor of the Yuan Dynasty) a supernatural omen showing Heaven's approval of the latter being the ruler of China in an attempt to find a new patron.

After unifying China, Kublai Khan rewarded Master Zhang a second-rank silver seal for the meritorious service he had performed in transmitting the omen, and assigned him to take charge of Taoist religious affairs south of the Yangtze River. Since then the succeeding emperors of the Yuan Dynasty all granted titles to Master Zhang as the first emperor Kublai Khan did. In 1353, the Masters from the fourth to thirty-fourth generations were all conferred a posthumous title of *Zhen Jun* (Taoist immortal title).

During the Ming period, Master Zhang had a high social status and rank of nobility. Before declaring himself emperor, Zhu Yuanzhang, born to a humble family, slaughtered large numbers of people. This always weighed on his conscience, and he feared that he would some day be punished by the divinity. Zhang Zhengchang, Master of the forty-second generation, sent for him a "memorial to Heaven," thus extricating him from the secret trouble. In 1373, the emperor assigned the Master a lifelong post to administer the Taoist religious affairs throughout the country. Emperor Shizong (r. 1522-1565), the most devout follower of the Taoist religion, cherished the illusion that he would become immortal. With unusual faith in Master Zhang's magic charms and prayers, the emperor issued as many as forty-one imperial orders and edicts to the priest during the forty-five years of his reign. He even granted the Master high favours when the latter married, had a son and at his death.

In the early period of the Qing Dynasty, Master Zhang was entitled to a hereditary rank of nobility following the Ming example. Emperor Shizong (r. 1723-1735) allocated 100,000 taels of silver for the extension of a Taoist Temple. However, the Qing rulers attached more importance to Buddhism than Taoism, and there were plenty of people in the court who were sceptical about Master Zhang and even against him. In 1752, during the reign of Emperor Qianlong, a censor seized on a mistake of Zhang Yulong, Master of the fifty-sixth generation, exposed his misdeeds and demoted him to the fifth of the nine ranks, hence greatly playing down his position and prestige. And the Five Pecks of Rice Sect began to decline.

Legends of Master Zhang

Master Zhang was a deified figure. Many legends were told about him. One said that Zhang Daoling was the eighth descendant of Zhang Liang, a high official of the Han Dynasty, and that he was a tall man, with an extraordinary appearance characterized by full forehead, red hair, green eyes, straight nose and square mouth, bushy eyebrows and big ears. His arms were so long that when he was standing his hands surpassed his knees. All this, plus his beard and martial gait, gave the impression that he looked like an immortal priest. In the tenth year of the Jianwu period under the reign of Emperor Guangwu of the Eastern Han Dynasty, he was born in Tianmu Mountain. Previously his mother dreamed about a tall immortal wearing a gold crown and embroidered robe descending from the Big Dipper to her room. He gave her a scented plant, and suddenly disappeared. She awakened to find that her quilt, clothes and the whole room sent forth an extraordinary fragrance which lingered for a month. Then she became pregnant. On the day when she was in labour, the courtyard was shrouded in coloured clouds, and the room was bright with red beams. The fragrance again filled the air. Daoling was able to walk as soon as he came to the world. With a glib tongue and extreme intelligence he had a good knowledge of *Dao De Jing* (*The Way and Its Virtue*), astronomy, geography and mystic diagrams at the age of seven. He passed the second-degree *xiaolian* in imperial examinations. Soon afterwards, he became the magistrate of Jingzhou. Though an official, he was determined to practise meditation. Before long he gave up the post and lived in seclusion in Beimang Mountain. It was said that one day a white tiger brought scriptures in its mouth to his table. Emperor He Di appointed him imperial tutor to the crown prince, and conferred on him the title Marquis of Jixian. He was invited to take up the official post three times, but he always refused. In A.D. 90, he went to Longhe Mountain in

Jiangxi Province where he tried to make pills of immortality and delivered sermons for about thirty years, his disciples totalling more than three thousand.

According to legend, during the reign of Emperor Shundi, Lord Lan Zi made it known that he passed Taoist magic tricks to Zhang Ling, taught him *Dao De Jing* and ordained him as Taoist Master, and founded Taoism. Thereafter, Zhang went to Sichuan and lived as a hermit on Heming (Singing Crane) Mountain. There on the picturesque mountain a stone crane sang from time to time. Each time it sang, someone would achieve the Way. Daoling devoted himself to self-discipline, and, together with his disciple Wang Chang, tried to form "Dragon-Tiger Pills." In one year, his room was illuminated by red beams; in two years, a blue dragon and white tiger stayed around the furnace to protect it; and in three years the pills were formed. Zhang was now ninety but he looked like a thirty-year-old. Popularly known as "Zhang the Immortal," he cured disease with magic water.

One day, when coming to Songshan Mountain in Henan Province with his disciple Wang Chang, Zhang came across a venerable priest. The latter, clad in a silk robe, said, "There is a stone room in the mountain where three alchemy classics were preserved. Try to get them and practise self-cultivation according to their instructions, and you will go up to Heaven." After fasting for seven days,

Zhang entered the stone room, dug up the floor and found the alchemy books under a stone slab. Painstakingly he cultivated the Way, and later became so fleet-footed that people had difficulty keeping up with him. He often went boating on a lake, or chanted scriptures on a terrace, or stayed home to entertain guests, or recited while strolling with a staff in hand. These activities of his could not be seen or heard by ordinary people.

In a village in today's Xinjiang there appeared an evil White-Tiger Deity, which was fond of drinking human blood. Every year someone had to be killed as a sacrifice to it. Zhang summoned the deity and warned it not to do any harm to the people. After that, tranquility and peace reigned over the place again.

A giant snake appeared in Zizhou. It spurted poisonous gas to kill pedestrians. Zhang conquered it with magic tricks for the benefit of the local people.

On the night of the fifteenth day of the first lunar month in 142 during the reign of Emperor Shundi, Zhang suddenly saw fragrant flowers covering the ground, and an auspicious cloud in the air. Amid the cloud, there was a plain carriage drawn by a white horse and escorted by figures with flags and banners. Sitting straight in the carriage was a tall, bearded man with a fair yellowish complexion and a halo around his head. Carrying a precious fan in his hand, he said, "Don't be frightened. I'm Lord Lao Zi."

Zhang prostrated himself to show his respect. Lao Zi gave him a copy of *San Dong Jing Lu (Canon of Three Caves)*, a pair of swords, a jade seal and a suit of clothes. After that, he began to read mysterious writings and practise meditation according to what was instructed in the book. In ten hundred days, he was able to see vital organs of the human body, and summon 36,000 deities. The fairy damsel taught him how to exhale and inhale pure and clean *qi* (air or vital energy) to subdue evil spirits. One day, the Jade Emperor announced that Zhang Daoling was to be conferred the title of "Zhengyi Zhenren."

Another legend says that Zhang Daoling was versed in the Five Classics. During the reign of Emperor Shundi of the Eastern Han Dynasty, witnessing the court growing more and more corrupt, he left his official post to visit famous mountains and seek the ideal of life. Afterwards, he took his disciples to Huming (Singing Swan) Mountain in Sichuan where he lived in seclusion, practised self-cultivation and wrote books about Taoism. It was his concentration on going into self-discipline that moved Li Zhijun, who taught him the way of the Zhengyi Sect to drive away demons and monsters, help the good and suppress the evil, and differentiate the human being from the ghost. Bringing with him the secret charms, he came to the evergreen Qingcheng Mountain.

As it happened, a monster was haunting the Qingcheng Mountain area harassing the local people and gobbling up their domestic animals. Master Zhang became furious upon learning about the monster's evil doings, and got rid of it immediately. Centuries later, when people take a walk from behind the Master Cave to the Longqiao Plank Road, they can see the Throwing-Brush Trough, a chasm sixty metres deep and twenty metres wide on the opposite steep cliff, which split the mountain into two right from the top to the bottom. The trough, according to legend, was the stroke made by Master Zhang with a writing brush to force the monster never to make trouble again. At the foot of a precipice at the back of the Master Cave, stands a huge rock, which, tradition claims, was split into two parts when the Master hacked it with a sword to conquer the monster. One part was again split into two, hence the name "Three-Isle Rock." The two-character inscription on the rock, meaning "Conquering the Monster," was carved by the descendant of the sixty-first generation of Master Zhang when he came to Qingcheng Mountain to pay homage to his ancestor in 1883 during the reign of Qing Emperor Guangxu.

Master Zhang was said to have cured diseases with magic water and incantations, and delivered people from danger and disaster. He taught them to help others, led them in building roads, reclaiming the land and removing filth. He also built a pond outside the temple to provide birds and animals with drinking water. The Master Cave was the place where he had preached, but the temple was built in his memory by people who came after. It was first constructed in the Sui Dynasty, and rebuilt later several times. Today's magnificent structure was built in late Qing. In a cave at the back of the temple stands a stone statue of Master Zhang for devout believers or tourists to pay homage.

Master Zhang's descendants came in sixty-three generations in about two millennia. They were conferred titles generation after generation by emperors. Particularly during and after the Song Dynasty, many times they were invited to the capital city and feted by the emperors themselves, and rewarded with high position and handsome salary. On top of that, at Shangqingzhen in today's Guixi County, Jiangxi Province, they built for themselves a magnificent temple, which, like a government office, was provided with judges, guards, secretaries, dispatchers and purchasing agents. They could ordain leading priests in various provinces, and set up a tribunal to exercise their right to interrogate and decide cases.

On inspection tours the Master always wore a dragon robe and rode a large sedan chair, with warriors in front to clear the way and the temple guards following behind. On both sides were people with placards and banners and a band piping and drumming. If yellow silk sunshades and imperial concubines were included in the procession, people would have thought that His Majesty was coming.

Master Zhang of various dynasties not only owned several thousand *mu* of land, but, beginning from the Song Dynasty, was immune from agricultural tax with the approval of the emperor. He defrauded people of large amounts of money by selling charms, holy water and elixir to "cure disease," performing Taoist rites "to save the souls of the dead," and practising usury. Master Zhang of a later generation had organized reactionary armed forces to suppress a peasants' uprising.

"There is nothing to be afraid of when there is no way to Heaven," as a proverb runs, "but it is really terrifying when Master Zhang becomes bewitched." This shows the sceptical attitude of the common people towards the efficacy of Master Zhang's magic tricks. In 1949, the Master Zhang of the last generation ran away from his traditional residence in Longhu Mountain to Guangzhou where he lived by making "efficacious charms." On the eve of the liberation of the city, this so-called immortal, awed by the power of the people, sought safety in flight.

ANCESTRAL EMPEROR—
LORD LAO ZI

From Lao Zi to Lord Lao Zi

Lao Zi, also known as Lao Dan, was a real historical figure. According to *Records of the Historian*, Lao Zi was born Li Er, a thinker of the Spring and Autumn Period and founder of the Taoist school of thought. The exact dates of his life were unknown, except that he was well over twenty years older than Confucius. For political reasons, he sought asylum in the State of Lu. Confucius, then seventeen years old, paid a visit to him asking for his views about the Zhou rites. Coming from a declining aristocrat's family of the lower stratum, he worked as keeper of books for the Zhou court. Distressed at the decline of the dynasty, he returned to his hometown and lived there as a hermit. There is a story that Lao Zi in his late years rode a black ox to travel westward through Hangu Pass in western Shaanxi Province. At the pass he was stopped by a guard, who asked Lao Zi to write down his thoughts in book form. The volume he was said to have written is known as the five-thousand-character *Book of Lao*

Ancestral Emperor—Lord Lao Zi

Zi, or *Dao De Jing* (*The Way and Its Virtue*). After he finished the book, he went on his trip to the State of Qin. He died at Fufeng (southeast of today's Xingping County in Shaanxi Province) and was buried at Huaili, administration centre of Fufeng.

The Book of Lao Zi, a philosophical work of the pre-Qin period with a widespread influence, has been hitherto considered a classic of Taoism. It contains eighty-one chapters in two parts dealing with "Tao" or "Dao" (the Way) and "De" (Virtue), hence the name *Dao De Jing of Lao Zi*. Many editions have been handed down from the Han Dynasty, but with discrepancies among them in content and language. The one in common use has the *Dao Jing* as the first part, and the *De Jing* as the second. However, in *The Book of Lao Zi* copied on silk unearthed in 1973 from Han Tomb No. 3 at Mawangdui in Changsha, Hunan Province, the *De Jing* is placed before the *Dao Jing*. This probably is the edition most like the original edition of ancient times. Though the book was completed during the early Warring States Period, there has been a controversy over who its author is—Lao Zi or someone else of later times. Most scholars believe that *The Book of Lao Zi* was not written by Lao Dan himself, but that one thing is definite; that is, it contains his main ideas.

The two versions of the book uncovered in 1973 at Mawangdui in Changsha have now been collated and published, which has aroused a new understanding of the position of Lao Zi's philosophical work in history. Some scholars hold that *The Book of Lao Zi* is a book dealing with military strategy and tactics. It is not a work by a strategist, but a philosophical work on the art of war by a philosopher.

According to Lao Zi, all things in the universe come out of the same origin, which he called Tao or *wu* (nonexistence). There are two opposite forces which coexist in a thing. The development of the thing is the result of interaction of the two opposite forces. Of the two, one is strong and the other is weak. In the course of development of a thing, the weak will always triumph over the strong.

During the Eastern Han period, with the spread of Buddhism to China, some sorcerers mixed the elements of Lao Zi's teachings with the original religious beliefs based on witchcraft to develop a new religion—Taoism. As a result, Lao Zi was made the prominent Lord Lao Zi of the religion, who, after being "processed," was more and more different from what he was originally like.

Lord Lao and Taiqing Temple

The Records of Henan Province notes that Taiqing Temple lies five kilometres east of Henan Province's Luyi County (formerly known as Kuxian of the State of Chu), hometown of Lao Zi, the founder of the Taoist school of thought. Taiqing

(Great Purity), referring to the heavens where, tradition claims, immortals resided, was often used by Taoist believers to name their temples. Taiqing Temple, first built sometime between 158 and 167 in the Eastern Han Dynasty, was repaired many times in later dynasties. The extant hall was rebuilt in early Qing times. At the former site stand two well-preserved, magnificent steles, one from the Tang Dynasty bearing the text of *Dao De Jing*, the other with inscriptions by Emperor Zhenzong of the Song Dynasty. There are also steles with inscriptions from the Yuan, Ming and Qing dynasties. At the northeastern corner of the county seat is Laojun Terrace, where legend says Lao Zi attained immortality. Laojun (Lord Lao Zi) Terrace, also known as Shengxian (Becoming Immortal) Terrace or Baixian (Worshipping Immortal) Terrace, is a thirteen-metre-high cylindrical structure with a terrace at the top. On the terrace are a three-room hall, with two short steles set in its walls, and a dozen hardy, towering old cypresses. At the main temple gate stands a stele bearing the text of *Dao De Jing* and its annotations, which was believed to have been erected by a Tang emperor. The stele is three metres high and one metre wide with a semi-circular top and a tortoise as its base. Inscriptions on both sides are in the *lishu* (official script) style. Each side contains twenty-two lines, each line consisting of twenty-one characters. Through centuries of weathering, more than half the inscriptions are illegible. But in view of the annotations made by a Tang emperor for *Dao De Jing*, and the remnant text, the stele is still listed among China's rare cultural relics.

In the Tang Dynasty, Li Yuan (Emperor Gaozu, 618-626) and his son Li Shimin (Emperor Taizong, 627-649) went even further in venerating Lord Lao Zi. As Lao Zi was surnamed Li, the two emperors granted him a posthumous title "First Ancestor." During the Wude period of Gaozu's reign, the emperor ordered General Yuchi Gong to supervise the construction of temples for the First Ancestor. According to ancient literature, the two temples —Taiqing and Dongxiao—were so magnificently built that they could compare with an imperial palace. Dongxiao was the estate of Lao Zi's mother, a place for Taoist nuns to live, and Taiqing was the fief of Lao Zi. The two were separated by a small river spanned by the Yuxian (Meeting Immortals) Bridge. In 666 Emperor Gaozong titled Lao Zi "Emperor Taishang Xuanyuan" and later "Emperor Hunyuan Shangde," making Taiqing Temple the ancestral temple of the imperial Li family.

Why Tang Emperors Held Lao Zi in Esteem

Tang emperors held Lao Zi in esteem because Li Yuan and his son Li Shimin believed that the god surnamed Li would certainly support the imperial court of the Lis and also because they wanted to take advantage of this honoured name to win people's support by any means. History says that in the fifth lunar month of the third year of the Wude period in 620, Li Yuan spread a myth, which goes like this: Ji Shanxing, a native of Jinzhou (today's Linfen County in Shanxi Province), met an old man of a sage-like type. Coming up on a vermilion-maned white horse, the latter said, "Please tell the emperor of the Tang Dynasty that I am his ancestor. If the rebels are quelled this year, our descendants can enjoy the reign for a thousand years." Li Yuan and Li Shimin energetically publicized the tale not only to show that they had Lao Zi as their ancestor, but that they had gained the support from a deity in an attempt to lend impetus and strength, and to dupe the people. They worshipped Taoism so that it grew even more flourishing. They built temples in memory of Lao Zi and held ceremonies for offering sacrifices and praying to him. They changed Fushan County (where the elderly sage left his message for Li Yuan) into Shenshan (Divine Mountain) County and granted Ji Shanxing the title *Dafu* (a senior official).

As a matter of fact, Li Yuan and Lao Zi, though both with the surname Li, did not belong to the same clan. Therefore, it was groundless to claim that Lao Zi was the ancestor of the imperial Li family. Moreover, Lao Zi lived at a time at least nine hundred years earlier than early Tang. Then, how could he talk with Ji Shanxing in the third year of the Wude period?

In mid-Tang, Li Longji (Emperor Xuanzong, 712-741) spread a tale that he dreamed about Lord Lao Zi and ordered that Lao Zi's "true features" be portrayed and promulgated throughout the country. He also issued an edict containing a series of political measures. Particularly worth mentioning was the addition of Taoist classics to form the core of the subjects to be tested in the imperial examinations. Consequently the Tang court worshipped Taoism as the state church and venerated Lao Zi as Deity of the Way and Virtue, Tianzun, one of the Three Pure Deities, and Emperor the Patriarch.

Towards the end of the Tang Dynasty, the insurrectionary army led by Huang Chao came to Taiqing Temple and set fire to this "imperial family temple" of the Tang court to reduce it to ashes. Reconstruction and repair were made by Taoist devotees during the centuries that followed, but the temple could never be restored to its original splendour. What remains now is a hall, some ancient cypresses, iron columns and steles. Despite this, those influenced by feudal ideology still take it as a sacred place and come there praying for good luck.

JADE EMPEROR —
THE HIGHEST RULER IN
HEAVEN

The Jade Emperor was believed to be the highest ruler of all gods in Heaven. As he was created by men later than other gods, his statue did not appear until the Tang Dynasty when the rulers of the lower world began to feel the necessity to create a supreme ruler with divine right, the Jade Emperor, to systematize their religious authority and tighten their spiritual control over the people.

Since the Yin and Zhou times, the belief in the highest deity, the Heavenly Emperor, had been widespread. In pre-Qin literature a number of terms for the highest god were referred to—such as *Tian* (Heaven), *Huangtian* (Heaven), *Di* (Emperor), *Tiandi* (Heavenly Emperor), etc. As the division of labour in society became more elaborate, and social organization and social consciousness became more complicated, so the world of spirits and gods was rigidly stratified. During the Western Han period, there were the Emperor of the Five Regions, *Taiyi* (Heavenly God), the North Star (believed to be the Heav-

Jade Emperor—the Highest Ruler in Heaven

enly Emperor'), etc. But, when there was a grand ceremony for rendering homage to Heaven, the Heavenly Emperor was the main deity to be worshipped. After the Eastern Han Dynasty, the primitive Heavenly Emperor was still being worshipped by emperors of various dynasties during the grand ceremonies for offering sacrifices to gods. Under the ever extending influence of Taoism and Buddhism, however, more and more people accepted the deities of the two religions.

The Heavenly Emperor became more and more personified and socialized among the people in their beliefs. He was gradually divorced from the abstract concept in the official ceremonies for offering sacrifices.

The Tang rulers made Taoism the state church, which completed and systematized the rule by divine power. Many Taoists of the upper strata held that, as there was an emperor in the lower world, so there should be a supreme ruler in Heaven as well, and a Jade Emperor was thus created. In ancient times, a story says, there existed a state. The King was getting old but still without a son. He prayed to Lord Lao Zi for one to inherit his throne. Soon after, the empress dreamed about the lord coming to her palace with a baby in his arms. Then she became pregnant and gave birth to a baby boy. When growing up, the heir unexpectedly gave up his throne, distributed all his property and went to a mountain to cultivate himself according to Taoist doctrine. He assisted the state and helped people in peril. Experiencing 3,200 *kalpas*, he first proved himself to be the Buddha, and after a hundred million more *kalpas*, to become the Jade Emperor —the supreme deity in Heaven and the loftiest emperor of the world of spirits and gods. This myth served to identify the Jade Emperor in Heaven with the crown prince of the lower world, thus in the main identifying the divine power with the monarchical authority.

The birthday of the Jade Emperor fell on the ninth day of the first lunar month. According to Wang Kui, the odd numbers, or the numbers of the *yang* category, start from one and end with nine. This explains why the birthday of the Jade Emperor was set on such a date. Wang Kui, a native of Qiantang, Zhejiang Province, was a poor intellectual, lame in one leg. He sold medicine to eke out his livelihood. Still he could not get enough to eat, so he often practised divination for others. Sick and tired of living this way, he began to study hard and gradually accumulated a wealth of knowledge, which enabled him to write books and set forth his views in his late years. His explanation about the Jade Emperor's birthday also involved the consideration that the ninth day of the first lunar month corresponded with the first solar term—the Beginning of Spring.

Although the Jade Emperor came later than other gods, because of his supreme position he became their father or grandfather. The Kitchen God, for instance, had been worshipped before the Spring and Autumn and the Warring States periods. And God Erlang was venerated during the Han Dynasty. Both had their temples more than ten centuries earlier than the Jade Emperor. However, the Kitchen God was made the youngest son of the Jade Emperor, and God Erlang was demoted to be the Emperor's nephew.

There is a folk tale about the origin of "Jade Emperor Zhang." It runs: The gods in Heaven, unwilling to acknowledge each other's superiority, always fought each other, and this caused confusion in the lower world. To remedy the situation, several heavenly deities enjoying prestige and commanding universal respect decided to choose someone with ability and integrity as emperor of the three worlds —Heaven, the lower world and the underworld. The Great White Planet and Lord Lao Zi called the gods together to consult them on how to select one enjoying the trust of all. At the meeting, the Wind God, Fire God, Thunder God and many others volunteered to be the candidate. Reluctant to give up, they almost started a fight. Finally they agreed with the Great White Planet's proposal to look for a suitable person in the lower world and entrust him with the task.

The Great White Planet transformed himself into a beggar coming down to the world of men. Clad in ragged clothes, he looked unusually ugly. He did not beg rice, nor money. The only thing he asked for was a bowl of inexhaustible ginseng soup, a request which nobody could fulfil. He insisted on begging the ginseng soup disregarding his stomach rumbling with hunger.

One morning, the beggar came to Zhangjiawan, where he found the local people different from those in other places—men were working in the fields and women plying the loom. Villagers, old and young, lived on good terms. The rich were held in esteem, while the poor were not bullied. The beggar was sure there must be a capable person who had run the village so well that it was even better than the paradise. Then he found the village head, Zhang Youren, also known as Zhang Bairen (tolerating everything), a gracious name given by the local people for his forbearing and conciliatory attitude towards everything. Because he treated people as equals and helped the distressed and succoured those in peril, he was also called "Great Benefactor."

The beggar decided to go and see what the person was really like. When he came to the entrance of Zhang Bairen's house, he was so hungry that he fainted. Zhang carried him on his back to his own bed and saved him. But he refused to drink tea, asking instead for ginseng soup. Zhang did not show impatience, but cooked a large bowl of ginseng soup for him. The beggar lived together with Zhang for fifteen days and was treated like a kinsman. Then he was convinced that Zhang was a great benefactor in the very real sense.

One day, the beggar said, "I am the Great White Planet from the upper world. Now I have come down to the lower world to look for a qualified person. Because you behave yourself very well, I want to invite you to go up to Heaven to be the emperor." Zhang refused but was forced to fulfil his request. Together with him, Zhang brought to Heaven not only his wife (later popularly called Queen Mother of the West) and his seven daughters, but also his chickens, ducks, cats, dogs and the wife's peach orchard. To run the three worlds well, Zhang conscientiously dealt with the state affairs. He started using intelligent and talented people, and respected all officials, major or minor. He often asked and learned from his subordinates without feeling ashamed. Within a few months, he obtained a good knowledge of the situation in the three worlds and found out the root cause for the great chaos there.

Seeing that Zhang Bairen was able to remedy the chaotic situation, veteran ministers such as the Great White Planet and the Pagoda-Bearing Heavenly King Li all did their best to assist the government. Several years later, the heavens, the lower world and the underworld were set in perfect order.

Zhang was not complacent over the achievements he had made, nor intoxicated with self-satisfaction amidst a shower of praise. He remained modest and prudent, and solicited different views.

All the humans, gods, spirits and monsters who had contacts with him were overwhelmed with his talent. They presented petitions or memorials demanding Zhang Bairen be made a life-long Heavenly Emperor. Since then Zhang had become an emperor who would never abdicate. As a sovereign of this sort would remain unchanged like a jade statue, he was named "Jade Emperor." Besides, he was the emperor of the three worlds, so he was also called the "Great Emperor."

THE QUEEN MOTHER OF
THE WEST

The Queen Mother of the West worshipped in many places was portrayed as an elegant, poised and loving mother, flanked by six ladies, two delivering a baby boy, two approaching childbirth, and two treating communicable measles. She also looked like a compassionate and merciful bodhisattva. Many people just worshipped a strip of yellow or red paper with words reading, "The Spirit Tablet of the Queen Mother of the West," in the hope that misfortune could be averted, good luck and longevity be blessed and babies be protected.

According to the *Classic of Mountains and Rivers*, the Queen Mother, on the whole looking like a human, was actually a fierce monster in charge of pestilence and punishment. She had tiger teeth, a leopard tail and dishevelled hair ornamented with jewels. She lived in a cave-dwelling in the wilderness and was good at howling.

In some other ancient books the Queen Mother was described as a beautiful goddess. In the *Biography of King Mu*, for instance, she was an elegant, gentle, kind-hearted goddess who could sing songs

西王母

The Queen Mother of the West

and write poems. At a banquet she and King Mu of the Zhou Dynasty replied to each other by reciting poems. The book went on to say that the king rode on a steed to the Jade Pool in the Kunlun Mountains where he was entertained by the Queen Mother. The latter also travelled eastward to pay a return visit. King Mu received her in Zhao Palace as a distinguished guest.

In another ancient book, *Stories of Emperor Wudi of the Han Dynasty*, the Queen Mother is also depicted as a beautiful, graceful young goddess followed by a large group of fairy maidens in attendance. One year on the seventh evening of the seventh lunar month, the book says, Emperor Wudi met with the Queen Mother, who brought three peaches of immortality to him as a present. The tale of Emperor Wudi meeting with the Queen Mother was told to raise the social status of the ruler by dint of the prestige of the goddess in charge of pestilence and punishment, though described as a monster in the *Classic of Mountains and Rivers*. Of course, it was based on the *Biography of King Mu* that the myth was turned into a fairy tale. It was also based on this book that the Queen Mother was established as a female celestial. In a later book, *Anecdotes of Emperor Wudi of the Han Dynasty* by Ban Gu, the Queen Mother became a goddess queen, an exceedingly beautiful young woman. Still later, the Taoists worshipped the Queen Mother as the leading deity in charge of the register of female immortals.

The available data shows that the Queen Mother of the West was first worshipped around the Qilian Mountains in the northwest. By the Spring and Autumn and the Warring States periods, legends of the goddess had been widespread in the Central Plains. No matter what the origin and implications, she had been made a deity in the eyes of the Chinese people prior to the Warring States Period. Since then, tales about the Queen Mother in charge of immortality elixir had been circulated. In the Qin and Han periods, when the emperors were all keen on searching for such a medicine and the art of gaining immortality, the Queen Mother was described as a white-haired immortal (*Myths and Facts in Ancient China*). She was worshipped as a major deity towards the end of the Western Han Dynasty. During the Eastern Han Dynasty, in view of the influence of the Queen Mother among the people, the newly-emerging Taoism naturally would take her in as one of its deities. In later times, Taoist priests and scholars, adding fuel to the flames, made her the daughter of *Yuanshi Tianzun* (Supreme Heavenly God), who, a celestial beauty in her thirties, was married to the Prince of the East. The temples to her name could be found almost all over the country. Some time later, the myth inventors again made her the wife of the Jade Emperor when he became the idol of worship. Then came the "celebrations of her birthday," "peach feast," etc. The

Queen Mother appears as a very important goddess in Taoist classics, novels about gods and devils, and folk tales.

LORD ZHENWU—
DEITY OF THE NORTH

Zhenwu Temple was to be found almost everywhere in China in the old days. In the Qing Dynasty in Beijing, for instance, Zhenwu Temple, together with Local God Temple, ranked third in the number of temples, only after Lord Guan and Goddess of Mercy temples. All told there were more than forty Zhenwu temples in Beijing and fifteen streets and lanes named after him. In Foshan, Guangdong Province, there is also a magnificent temple dedicated to him. First built in 1078-1085 as a shrine for the founders of various trades and professions, it was turned into a temple to Lord Zhenwu in 1372, when it was rebuilt. The bronze statue of the god was cast in 1452 and weighs 2,500 kilogrammes. It sits upright, one hand on one knee and the other hand tugging at a jade belt, his face wearing a solemn look. Believed to be the commander of trouble-making tortoises, snakes, fish and turtles, he is worshipped in Foshan and other places in the Pearl River Delta, where floods are frequent, in the hope that he would rid the areas of floods.

Lord Zhenwu—Deity of the North

Lord Zhenwu (True Martiality) was the Deity of the North in ancient mythology, also known as North Lord Zhenwu, Lord Black or Xuanwu (Black Martiality). A Taoist temple in Wudang Mountain in Junxian County, Hubei Province, is specially devoted to the worship of Lord Zhenwu. The statue with dishevelled hair is dressed in black, holding a sword in hand and stepping on a snake and tortoise. On both sides stand attendants with black flags in hand. Zhenwu's statues are varied: some dressed like a boy, some attired like a youth, and others seated properly just like one who has attained immortality.

Versions are different about the origin of Lord Zhenwu. To begin with, the term Xuanwu, which, according to *Elegies of Chu* by Qu Yuan (c. 340-278 B.C.), statesman of the State of Chu in the Warring States Period, "is the name for the God of the North" and "Xuanwu means the tortoise and snake." This shows that at that time he was not a human, but a god.

In 1012, Zhao Heng, Northern Song Dynasty Emperor Zhenzong, a devout follower of Taoism, dreamed about Zhao Yuanlang. The latter said he was one of the nine Renhuang (emperor of the lower world) brothers and also the earliest ancestor of the Zhao clan. Later he was born to the human world again as Emperor Xuanyuan, and then came to the world of men the third time in the Tang Dynasty as head of the Zhao clan. He advised the Song emperor to take good care of the people. Based on the dream, the emperor granted the nonexistent Zhao Yuanlang the title "Emperor Shengzu." To avoid a taboo, the name "Xuanwu" for the God of the North was changed to "Zhenwu." During the period between 1008 and 1016, the god was honoured as "Lord Zhenwu."'

In 1017 a soldier discovered a tortoise and a snake. This was nothing special, but Taoist priests stubbornly insisted that Lord Zhenwu had shown his bodily presence. Hence a temple to Zhenwu was built to enshrine the god of tortoise and snake.

A taoist tale goes that Zhenwu was the Crown Prince of the Kingdom of Pure Happiness. Born bold and powerful, he crossed the East Sea on a tour and came upon the Heavenly God Yuqing Shengzu, who gave him a sword, taught him the Way, and told him to go to Taihe Mountain to practise meditation. Forty-two years later Zhenwu attained immortality and went up to Heaven in daytime, where he accepted the title Xuanwu from the Jade Emperor. Hereafter, Taihe Mountain was renamed Wudang Mountain, meaning only Xuanwu deserves it.

In the Yongle period of the Ming Dynasty, to consolidate his rule, Zhu Di (r. 1403-1424) made use of Wudang Mountain to personify the god Zhenwu.

After becoming emperor, Zhu Di claimed he was Lord Zhenwu reincarnate. So, he mobilized more than 300,000 soldiers and civilians to build in Wudang Mountain hundreds of magnificent Taoist temples and nunneries in a decade to show his mighty power. However, Taoist priests in the mountain did not believe in the lies of Zhu Di. They said to the visitors, "The master priest of the mountain was Emperor Jianwen (r. 1399-1402) reincarnate. So all the halls in the mountain were built after the pattern of the imperial palace." In other words, they did not accept Zhu Di as Lord Zhenwu in transmigration. They said Lord Zhenwu was the Crown Prince of the Kingdom of Pure Happiness. When cultivating the Way here, he lived in what is now called Taizipo (Crown Prince Slope). For this reason, a magnificent Fuzhen (Return to the True) Temple was built there, with one huge column supporting twelve beams, a rare masterpiece in ancient architecture.

In the hall in a stone cave behind Zixiao Palace, the largest one in the mountain, was enshrined the stone statue of a young man, with a plump and smooth-skinned face and elegant bearing. According to the Taoist priests, he was the Crown Prince of the Kingdom of Pure Happiness, hence the stone cave bears the name of Taiziyan (Crown Prince Cave).

In another legend made up by the priests, the crown prince, tired of meditating alone in the mountain to attain immortality, decided to go back to the world of men. On his way down, he came upon an old woman beside a well, grinding away at a thick iron bar. "What are you doing?" the prince inquired. "Making a needle," she said.

"When could you finish it?"

"Constant effort yields sure success," she replied

Chastened, the prince went back to his meditation in the mountain, and finally achieved immortality. The Taoist followers built a complex of temple buildings called Mozhenjing (Grinding Needle Well). On the left side is a hall housing a seated statue of Lord Zhenwu in his youth. Down below the flight of steps in front of the hall stand two large iron bars. On the right side is Laomu Ting (Old Mother Pavilion), a square pavilion with overhanging eaves. Inside lies the Grinding Needle Well.

In large Taoist temples in Wudang Mountain are enshrined the statues of Lord Zhenwu, Lord Yuan, the Jade Emperor, and the Three Pure Deities. About the Five-Dragon Palace, a story goes like this: During the Zhenguan period (627-649) of the Tang Dynasty, Yao Jian, prefect of Junzhou (today's Junxian County), when praying for rain, suddenly saw five dragons descending from the heavens. A few minutes later, the rain was pelting down. Hence a palace hall was built as a memento of this incident. Ironically, this great temple did not escape attack by the Fire God, and most of its buildings were destroyed at the end of the Yuan Dynasty. The statues of the Water God and Lord Zhenwu, after enjoying several hundred years of worship, failed to overcome a fire.

The Taoist priests also designed a place where Lord Zhenwu was said to have attained immortality —Feisheng Tai (Flying-to-Heaven Terrace) at Nan-

yan (Southern Rock), five kilometres west of the
Zixiao Palace in Wudang Mountain. Nanyan is set
on a steep cliff long known for its tranquility. It
features a temple building, Tianyi Zhenqing Palace
—a stone hall carved out of a living rock in imita-
tion of the customary wooden architecture. The
Flying-to-Heaven Terrace, where Lord Zhenwu was
said to have soared to Heaven, is located west of the
Stone Hall. Some devotees, at the risk of their lives,
went to the tip of a stone beam carved with cloud
designs and protruding over the edge of the cliff to
burn joss sticks in worship of Lord Zhenwu.

As a matter of fact, Wudang Mountain is not
famed for the magic power of Lord Zhenwu, but for
the rich and exquisite bronze relics in the scattered
Taoist temples and the Wudang boxing style, which
has enjoyed equal popularity with Shaolin school of
boxing. The Wudang type, the best for resisting the
enemy, will not be used unless in a dangerous
situation, and one who has mastered the technique
will surely win.

The inventor of Wudang boxing was Zhang San-
feng, a Taoist priest in Wudang Mountain. By ob-
serving a magpie sporting with a snake, he created
the thirteen-movement *Taijiquan* which combined
meditation with motion. This was later developed
into the boxing style of twenty-two-movement *Taiyi Wuxing Qinpu* by Zhang Shouxing, the eighth-
generation master priest in Wudang Mountain. This
Wudang school of boxing enjoys popularity not

only at home, but also in Japan and Southeast Asian countries.

Tales and legends made Zhenwu highly noble and celebrated. However, he exerted the greatest influence as the Water God. During the Ming Qing period, his statues were enshrined in the palace buildings in the Forbidden City, and temples to his name were built in multi-level government offices of the Royal Household Department. Many merchants also worshipped Zhenwu to prevent fires.

KING TIANZHONG—
THE GOD OF SONGSHAN
MOUNTAIN

Songshan Mountain in Dengfeng County, Henan Province, also known as Zhongyue Songshan (Songshan in the Centre), is one of China's five sacred mountains. Tradition claims that these five mountains were haunts of immortals and that emperors in ancient times went to them to hold grand ceremonies to worship Heaven. Seventy-two emperors in history were said to have gone to Taishan to offer sacrifices, symbolizing the unification of the country and the unity of various nationalities. The fact that only the wise, virtuous emperors in times of prosperity were qualified to hold such ceremonies shows the importance of the five sacred mountains.

Taoist believers worshipped the five sacred mountains, holding that each had a mountain god. According to *Daozang Jiyao* (*Summary of Taoist Scriptures*), the God of Taishan in the East had the title of King Tianqi; the God of Hengshan in the South, King Sitian; the God of Huashan in the West,

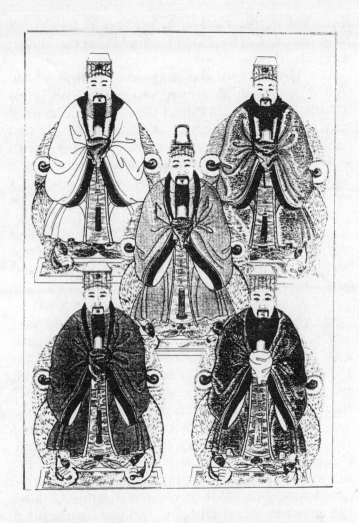

King Tianzhong—the God of Songshan Mountain

King Jintian; the God of Hengshan in the North, King Antian; and the God of Songshan in the Centre, King Tianzhong.

The Junji Hall of the Zhongyue Temple at the foot of Songshan Mountain houses the five-metre-tall statue of the Zhongyue God. It wears a royal crown and a golden robe, a ritual tablet in two hands—giving the impression that this is a god with grand airs. The *Taiping Miscellany*, a reference book with material taken from various sources, notes that the Zhongyue God was named Shou Yiqun, or General Songgao named Shi Yuanheng. *The History of the Zhongyue Temple* says that the Zhongyue God was named Yun Ying, who was in charge of the land and mountains as well as the feed for cows and sheep.

The Zhongyue God had long been honoured by rulers of many dynasties. The *Classic of Mountains and Rivers* describes him as having three heads, each with a human face, still considering him as a demi-god. The emperors of the Eastern Han Dynasty with its capital at Luoyang, Henan Province, frequently offered sacrifices to the long-personified god. To consolidate her own position, Empress Wu Zetian of the Tang Dynasty conferred on him first the title Shenyue (Divine Mountain), then King Tianzhong, and then emperor, making him the first of the five sacred mountain gods to receive the title of king and emperor. When Emperor Zhongzong ascended the throne, he cancelled the title of emperor. Later

Emperor Xuanzong changed King Tianzhong to King Zhongtian. He first gave a kingly title to Huashan Mountain in the west, then titled the gods of the other four sacred mountains king in a bid to prevail over Empress Wu Zetian's influence in spreading the idea that "the monarchical power is invested by Heaven." However, for historical and traditional reasons, the position and influence of Songshan Mountain has always remained lower than Taishan Mountain in the east.

THE THREE OFFICIALS TEMPLE AND THE THREE EMPERORS OF SHANGYUAN, ZHONGYUAN AND XIAYUAN

In the Three Officials Temples, the statues of Heavenly, Earthly and Water Officials, also known as Sanyuan Emperors, were enshrined. Their origin has direct connections with Taoism.

At a time when Taoism was promoted by the highest feudal rulers and became widespread among the people, Zhang Heng, son of Zhang Daoling, made up a story, *Notes by the Three Officials*, to the effect that man contracted diseases because he had committed sins. When falling ill, he claimed the patient did not have to call for a doctor, nor take medicine. What he was required to do for recovery was to write his name on three pieces of paper and to admit his guilt separately to the three officials. This story was later played up to associate the old Shangyuan (Upper Part of the Year) Festival (the fifteenth day of the first lunar month), Zhongyuan (Middle of the Year) Festival (the fifteenth day of the seventh lunar month) and Xiayuan (Lower Part.

The Three Emperors
of Shangyuan, Zhongyuan and Xiayuan

of the Year) Festival (the fifteenth day of the tenth lunar month)—collectively known as Sanyuan Festivals—with the three officials.

The three officials refer to the Shangyuan First-Rank Heavenly Official, Zhongyuan Second-Rank Earthly Official, and Xiayuan Third-Rank Water Official. As a step to get more people to worship them, the feudal rulers titled the Heavenly Official Emperor Ziwei in charge of "bestowing good luck," the Earthly Official Emperor Qingling in charge of matters of "absolution," and the Water Official Emperor Yanggu in charge of "eliminating adversities." The three emperors of Shangyuan, Zhongyuan and Xiayuan were thus created. Worshippers could pray to Emperor Ziwei for fame, wealth and good luck, to Emperor Qingling for absolution, and to Emperor Yanggu for avoidance of disasters.

During the Tang-Song period, the feudal ruling class was making still greater efforts to advance the domination of divine authority and tighten the spiritual trammels on the people, so the Three Officials Temples or Sanyuan Monasteries were erected everywhere across the country. In order to hoodwink the people and go along with the believers, the rulers showed their respect for the three gods. In the tenth lunar month of the twenty-second year of the Kaiyuan period of the Tang Dynasty, for instance, it was proclaimed that on the Sanyuan Festivals—the birthdays of the three heavenly emperors—slaughtering of draft animals was forbidden. The rulers of the Song Dynasty, at the suggestion of a Taoist priest, ordered that execution of criminals sentenced to death be suspended on the birthdays of the three deities.

Though the three gods were also made by men, nevertheless they enjoyed a rather high position in Taoism, and had an extensive influence among the people. Like the gods of the sun, the moon and the stars, they also originated in the primitive religion's worship of nature—heaven, earth and water.

THE GREAT SAGE EQUALLING HEAVEN

The Great Sage Equalling Heaven is the hero of the mythical novel *Journey to the West*, in which he is also called Sun Wukong, Sun Xingzhe (Sun the Novice) or Monkey King. He first storms the Heavenly Palace, then escorts the monk Xuan Zang of the Tang Dynasty to India to get Buddhist scriptures. With extraordinary power and infinite resourcefulness, he is well known in vanquishing elves and demons.

According to historical data, Fuzhou people all worshipped Sun Xingzhe and enshrined him in their homes. In addition, a Great Sage Equalling Heaven Monastery was established.

According to legend, a man from Yanzhou of Shandong Province, Xu Sheng, came to Fuzhou to do business with his brother Xu Cheng. They carried a large amount of goods, but sold out quickly. People envied their good luck and advised them: "That you are so smoothly selling your goods is due to the Great Sage's blessing. You'd better go to the monastery to express gratitude to him." Xu Sheng and his brother agreed and went to the magnificent monastery. Upon seeing the imposing statue with monkey head and human body, they hurried to burn joss sticks and candles, and prostrated themselves before the statue. Still another saying goes that Chaozhou in Guangdong also had a Great Sage Equalling Heaven Monastery attracting a large number of pilgrims.

Since the Great Sage is enshrined by so many good and honest people, what is his origin?

The Southern Song publication, *Poetic Notes on the Monk Xuan Zang of the Tang Dynasty Going to India for Buddhist Scriptures*, is a literary work based on historical facts. It contains fairy tales, including the legend on Hou Xingzhe (Monkey the Novice) following Xuan Zang to India to get Buddhist scriptures.

Hou Xingzhe called himself the King of the 84,000 bronze-head, iron-forehead monkeys of the Purple Clouds Cave on the Mountain of Flowers and Fruit. In the novel he was described as a hero with great power in subduing monsters and demons. But actuallly he was neither surnamed Sun nor addressed as "Great Sage Equalling Heaven." In the book *Poetic Notes* it was only mentioned that he was conferred the title, "Great Sage with Bronze Muscles and Iron Sinews," by Emperor Taizong of the Tang Dynasty.

The origin of Sun Wukong is briefed in the first seven chapters of the novel *Journey to the West* by Wu Cheng'en of the Ming Dynasty. This is the story:

At the edge of the country of Aolai, which is east of the ocean belonging to the Eastern Continent of Superior Body, there is the Mountain of Flowers and Fruit. A magic stone on the top of this mountain, nurtured by the favour of nature and irradiated by the rays of the sun and moon for ages, produced a stone egg, and when the wind blew on this egg, it turned into a stone monkey. He ate plants, drank brook water, and associated with wolves, tigers, panthers, deer and macaques. One day when bathing with a group of macaques in a mountain stream, he found a stone tablet carved with characters which read, "Water Curtain Cave of the Mountain of Flowers and Fruit." Therefore, they settled down there. All the macaques addressed the stone monkey "Great King." After ascending the "throne," he proclaimed himself "Handsome Monkey King" and led a carefree life everyday. Later, knowing that he was still under control of the King of Hell, Monkey King came to the Spirit Tower Mountain in Pengying across the Great Western Ocean where he took the Patriarch Subhut as his teacher to learn the way of immortality, then was given the Dharma-name Sun Wukong (Monkey Awakened to Emptiness). Because of his cleverness and diligence, he quickly mastered magical combat capabilities and was able to change himself into seventy-two different forms.

Turning a somersault he could cover a distance of 108,000 *li* (1 *li* =1/2 km). To obtain an extraordinary powerful weapon, he broke in the Dragon Palace and made Dragon King offer him a golden cudgel weighing 13,500 *jin* (1 *jin* = 1/2 kg) whose size could be changed as he wished. To rid himself of the control from the nether world, he rushed down to the Palace of Hell and forced the King of Hell to cancel all the records about the animals of the monkey family from the life-and-death register. On the way back to his mountain home, he slew the terrible Prince of Devils. His rebel acts infuriated the Jade Emperor, who originally intended to send troops to suppress him. But the Great White Planet worked out another plan and summoned Sun Wukong to Heaven to put him under control.

When meeting the Jade Emperor, Sun Wukong did not pay any respect or express his gratitude. The Jade Emperor made him Protector of the Horses. He was pleased, and took up his post enthusiastically, tending celestial horses. Later, when he learned that Protector of the Horses was but a petty official, he resented the Jade Emperor's looking down on him. Angrily he took the golden cudgel out of his ear. Armed with this powerful weapon, he broke out of the Southern Gate of Heaven and returned to his mountain den where he called himself "Great Sage Equalling Heaven" to show his opposition to the Heavenly Court. The Jade Emperor sent troops to arrest him. The Mighty Miracle God and Prince Ne Zha were defeated. Now Sun Wukong declared that the Jade Emperor should confer him the title, "Great

Sage Equalling Heaven," otherwise he would storm the Heavenly Palace. After failing to suppress him, the Jade Emperor ordered the Great White Planet to offer him amnesty, then conferred on him the title as he requested. This was done to keep him under control in Heaven. As a matter of fact, this was only an honorary appointment; he was not given any responsibility or paid any salary. Seeing Wukong loafing about the heavens all day long in an unconstrained manner, the Jade Emperor worried and sent him to be in charge of the Immortality Peach Garden. Wukong made use of his position as tender of the garden to choose those ripe and choice peaches to eat. When he was not invited to the Peach Feast given by the Queen Mother, he fooled the guard Barefoot Immortal by issuing an order in the name of the Queen Mother, and went straight to the Jade Pool where he ate and drank his fill. Inebrieted, he entered the Tushita Heavenly Palace of the Lord Lao Zi of the Great Monad. There he ate up all the elixir pills specially prepared for the Jade Emperor.

Unable to endure Wukong's defiant behaviour, the Jade Emperor sent 100,000 celestial soldiers to capture him. When this failed, the Jade Emperor assigned his nephew, the Illustrious Sage and True Lord Erlangzhenjun to fight Wukong. With help from the Goddess of Mercy, Erlangzhenjun finally captured Wukong. He was taken to the guillotine to be executed, but no sword could cut into his flesh. Fire and thunderbolts failed to hurt him. Lord Lao

Zi had him thrown into the Eight Trigrams Furnace to be calcined for forty-nine days. This did no harm to his body. On the contrary, his eyes became sharper than ever and could see anything invisible. As the furnace opened, he jumped out, kicking down the furnace and knocking down Lord Lao Zi. Flourishing his golden cudgel all the way, he burst into the Hall of Universal Brightness and broke out of the Hall of Miraculous Mist. The violence of his attack made the Nine Bright Shiners shut their doors and windows tight and the Four Heavenly Kings were also scared and disappeared.

The Jade Emperor had to request help from the Buddha. The Buddha turned his five fingers into a mountain chain belonging to the elements Metal, Wood, Water, Fire, and Earth, renamed them the Five Elements Mountain, and gently held him down. Under the mountain, Wukong allayed his hunger with iron balls, and quenched his thirst with copper juice. He had to wait for the saint monk of the Tang Dynasty to come to his rescue, then followed him to India to get Buddhist scriptures.

GOD ERLANG

Monasteries for God Erlang are found in many places in China. The one at Guankou in Guanxian County, Sichuan Province is the earliest. It was built in memory of Li Bing and his son, Erlang (meaning "Second Son"), for their remarkable work in construction of Dujiang Weir. But the gods enshrined in quite a few other monasteries are Yang Jian and Zhao Yu. In addition, Deng Xia of the Jin Dynasty, who was called the "hero killing flood dragon," and especially the second son of an Indian heavenly king, were also called God Erlang by some people.

God Erlang of Guankou

Over two thousand years ago, Li Bing, who had experience in regulating rivers and watercourses, was appointed governor of Sichuan, the highest local official.

Around Chengdu and Guanxian in the province is a large plain surrounded by mountains. The Min-jiang River begins in the snow-clad Minshan Moun-

二郎之位

God Erlang

tains in northwest Sichuan. Because the terrain on its upper reaches in very steep, the current rushes down vigorously. When reaching Guanxian where the terrain slopes gently, the current suddenly slowed down, and the silt was deposited. After a long period of time, the riverbed rose higher and higher. With the melting of the snow on the mountains in summer, the river invariably flooded its banks. How to prevent floods and guarantee good farm harvests was the pressing issue for the people around Guanxian in ancient times.

After taking up his post as the governor of Sichuan, Li Bing applied the experience of predecessors in harnessing rivers. He discovered the causes of flooding and sought ways of dealing with it. He ordered his son, Erlang, to be responsible for the construction of Dujiang Weir, then worked with him in leading the local people to complete the largest water control project in ancient China.

Although it was finished two thousand years ago, the planning, design and construction methods were highly scientific and creative. To meet the needs of irrigation and flood prevention, the project was built to regulate the water volume of the outer and inner rivers. During drought season, it could work for irrigation, and when rainy season came, the sluice gate was able to control the overflow. In short, the completion of Dujiang Weir made it possible to regulate water for farming all year round. This thoroughly changed the look of agricultural production of some ten counties around Chengdu Plain. An area frequently hit by flood and drought now became a vast expanse of fertile land and a huge granary. From then on, Chengdu Plain has been called the "Land of Abundance."

According to "Story About Li Bing and His Son in Harnessing Rivers" in *Records of Guanxian*, "After being appointed governor of Sichuan by King Zhao of the State of Qin, Li Bing channelled the water from the two rivers of Chengdu to irrigate thousands of hectares of farmland. His son Erlang helped him build water control works to prevent flood." A historical record says, "The Erlang Temple of Guankou in Sichuan was established in memory of Li Bing's merits in opening up salt wells, building bridges, developing the Guanxian area and Chengdu Plain, and promoting agricultural production. Many god pictures that appeared recently were the representation of the image of Li Bing's second son...." According to another story, "Having annexed Sichuan, the King of Qin appointed Li Bing governor of the area. Erlang went with him to Sichuan. At that time the area was frequently hit by floods. Erlang was ordered to find out the cause and to prevent it. From spring to winter he made long and difficult journeys, but failed to get any result. One day when going deep into a mountain, he encountered a tiger. Instantly, he killed it and cut its head off. At this moment came seven hunters, who were surprised at the sight of Erlang's bravery. Knowing

173

Erlang's task, they asked to go with him; Erlang agreed. As they approached a thatched cottage by a river near the county town of Guanxian, they heard somebody crying inside. They entered and found an old woman wailing for her youngest grandson who was to be taken away as a sacrificial offering for the river god—an evil dragon. Astounded, Erlang reported this to his father. Li Bing taught him how to capture the monster. On the sacrificial occasion, Erlang, holding his three-pointed and double-edged sword in hand, got into the River God Temple with his seven friends, and hid themselves behind the god statue. After a while, the dragon came with a gust of strong wind and heavy rain into the temple to snatch the oblation. Erlang and his mates jumped out immediately to fight it. Defeated, the dragon scurried out of the temple. Now, on the surrounding hills sounded the beating of gongs and drums and loud voices. This scared the dragon who fled to the river. To pursue it, Erlang and his mates dived into the river, too. At last, the dragon was captured. Being weary, Erlang and his mates took a rest under the Grandma Wang Crag and detained the dragon in the river. The river had a hole through which one could reach the Chongqingzhou River. Making use of this, the dragon escaped. Erlang and his mates at once plunged into the water to look for it, and finally put it under arrest at Tongzhiyan in Xinjin County. On returning to the Grandma Wang Crag, they met the old woman who had been grievously crying for her grandson. Now she came to express her gratitude and brought them an iron chain. With it, Erlang tied the dragon to a stone post of the Vanquishing Dragon Temple and had it detained in a deep pool. Since then, the area has been free of flood.

Here is another legend about Erlang with his seven friends vanquishing an evil dragon: Seven people were said to be the seven sages from Plum Mountain. But in a myth they were the spirits of monkey, pig, sheep, ox, dog, centipede and snake. Because they helped a tyrant king to do evil, they were killed by Yang Jian and Ne Zha. According to *The Chronicle of Chengdu Prefecture,* the seven people were all hunters and friends of Erlang. Some called them Seven Friends from Coal Mountain.* The mountain area around Guanxian County was a coal producer. So the seven people were probably coal miners of ancient times. In the past, the Erwang (Two Kings) Temple in Guanxian had the Seven Sages Hall in which the statues of the seven people were enshrined. Strange in appearance, they were also known as "Seven Monsters."

Today, when you enter the Erwang Temple, you will find a horizontal plaque above a small stage. It is a wooden carving with golden paint, probably made in early Qing Dynasty. This woodcut presents the scene of Erlang and his seven friends helping Li Bing to fight a rhinoceros.

---

* The Chinese characters for "plum" and "coal" are homophonic.

On the right is Li Bing, a strong bearded man who is fighting the wild beast with his hands. In the centre are eight warriors; one of them, the young man wearing helmet and armour, holding a three-pointed and double-edged sword, with hunting dogs around, is Erlang. The others are the "Seven Sages from Plum Mountain." The tale told above is a part of the legend about Erlang.

This is the story of Li Bing: After vanquishing the river god (namely the evil dragon), Li Bing made three stone figures at Baishayou, west of the county town, and placed them in the centre of the river. He and the river god reached this agreement: In dry season, the water level must not be lower than the feet of the stone figures, while in flood season it is not allowed to submerge their shoulders. In addition, Li Bing led the local people in making bamboo crates filled with stones to form a thirty-five-metre-long dam across the river, which was called Golden Dam and used for flood diversion. This eliminated the menace of flood and drought from then on. With numerous streams for irrigation, the vast plain has become so rich and fertile that people call it "Land of Abundance."

To commemorate the merits of Li Bing and his son Erlang in harnessing rivers, the stories about them were embellished with mythical colour. They were said to have become gods and were addressed, "God Erlang of Guankou." A temple was built to enshrine them at the foot of Yulei Mountain on the east bank of the Minjiang River. It was first named Chongde (Lofty Virtue) Temple. After the Song Dynasty, all emperors conferred on Li Bing and Erlang the title of king, so the original name was replaced by Erwang (Two Kings) Temple. But the people still called it "Erlang Temple." According to the quotations from Zhu Xi, a famous scholar of the Neo-Confucian school of the Song Dynasty, "The god enshrined in the Erlang Temple at Guankou in Sichuan is the second son of Li Bing." Another historical record reveals that in the fifth year during the reign of Emperor Yong Zheng of the Qing Dynasty, Li Bing was conferred the title "Fuzexingji-tongyou (Broad Beneficence and Blessing) King" and his son Erlang "Chengjiguanghuixianyin (Conspicuous Merits) King." Hence the temples for them were still called Erwang Temples. During the Southern and Northern Dynasties Period, an Emperor Wangdi Temple had been in existence in Guanxian County, and the god enshrined in it was Du Yu, a king of the ancient Shu (Sichuan) Kingdom who later claimed himself Emperor Wangdi. In the fifth year during the reign of Emperor Jianwu of the Southern Qi Dynasty, it was moved to Pixian County and named Chongde Temple, in which the god enshrined was Li Bing instead of Du Yu. In the Song Dynasty, the statue of Erlang was added in its front hall. The temple kept the same name.

At the northern end of Dujiang Weir an edifice called Vanquishing Dragon Temple was erected. It was said when working on harnessing rivers, Li Bing ordered his son Erlang to fight an evil dragon, and he subdued it.

The Erlang Gods—One Surnamed Zhao and the Other Deng

Apart from the preceding legends about God Erlang, there are another two, surnamed Zhao and Deng. According to historical records, a man named Zhao Yu from Sichuan was once a hermit in Mt. Qingcheng. Learning of his talents, Emperor Yangdi (569-618) of the Sui Dynasty appointed him head of Jiazhou (today's Leshan County of Sichuan Province). At that time, there was a flood dragon doing evil in the area. Amid deafening noise of drumbeats, firecrackers and cheers, Zhao Yu set out with ten hundred warriors to fight the dragon. Holding a double-edged sword in hand, Zhao Yu plunged into the water and killed the dragon. The water of the river was reddened by its blood. When Zhao Yu was out of the water, with the head of the dragon in his left hand and the double-edged sword in his right one, the local people all kneeled before him. Hence the establishment of a temple for him called "God Erlang of Guankou." *The Chronicle of Changshu County* says, "After the death of Zhao Yu of the Sui Dynasty, Jiazhou was hit by flood. The local people saw Zhao riding a white horse in the mist galloping across the currents. They built a temple by the Guanjiang River to enshrine him called "God Erlang of Guankou."

Another God Erlang was named Deng Xia, who surpassed others in valour. There was a saying, "The God Erlang Temple was located at Zhongqingli in Hangzhou City. Because Deng Xia killed a flood dragon, the area was no longer harmed. To express their gratitude, the local people set up the temple to enshrine him. He had once been a general under Erlang, so he was addressed, 'God Erlang.'"

Still another God Erlang was the second son of an Indian god, the Vaisravana Heavenly King. He frequently led troops from Heaven to guard their national boundaries. The third son Ne Zha always followed the Heavenly King, a pagoda in hand. He is a beloved hero in some Chinese mythical novels. The second prince was even more renowned in China. In the old days, foreign deities once introduced into China were often Sinicized. Therefore, Li Jing, a famous general of the early Tang Dynasty, was called "Heavenly King with a Pagoda in Hand" in the mythical novel *Journey to the West*, and the second Indian prince was named Yang Jian in the *Feng Shen Yan Yi* (*Romance of the Canonized Gods*) and was said to be Li Jing's nephew.

Of the different gods named Erlang mentioned

above, Li Bing's second son, Li Erlang, was the most influential, because he was honoured by all emperors since the Five Dynasties Period (907-960).

THE EIGHT IMMORTALS

$\mathcal{T}$he Eight Immortals are one of the most popular divine groups in China. Their names and images are seen in many places, and stories about them are illustrated in pictures, presented in plays and told in novels. Their portraits are also found on the sedan-chairs for carrying brides in rural areas, on the moulds for making cakes, and on the side corridor of the great hall of the City God Temple at Dongguan in Zhengzhou City.

The eight celestial beings in Taoism usually refer to Li Tieguai (Iron Crutch Li), Han Zhongli, Zhang Guolao, He Xiangu, Lan Caihe, Lü Dongbin, Han Xiangzi and Cao Guojiu.

Li Tieguai (Iron Crutch Li)

The first one of the Eight Immortals is Li Tieguai (Iron Crutch Li), also called Li Xuan. He often begged alms on the street, so people despised him.

He is a character popular in legend. With dishevelled hair and a dirty face, he was lame in one leg and used a crutch. Hence the nickname, Iron Crutch.

One story has it that he was originally smart and stalwart. One day when he set his soul out of his body to travel Huashan Mountain, he told his disciples that they would have to get his body cremated in case his soul did not come back within seven days. After the deadline, the disciples found their master's soul still absent, and were obliged to do as he had instructed. Soon afterwards, his soul returned and could not find his body. Then discovering the body of a dead man in a forest, he decided to attach himself to it. As he stood up, he felt something wrong with one leg. Taking the elixir presented by his teacher Lao Zi, he found himself becoming a man ugly in appearance. Lao Zi told him, "Outer appearance yields no influence over cultivation of Taoism. One would be a real celestial so long as he makes abundant achievements in merits and virtue."

Following is another legend about him:

At the foot of Laoshan Mountain there was a squire named Li. In addition to possessing hundreds of hectares of fertile farmland, he had a lot of gold and silver. But one thing which made him feel very sorry was that he did not have a son even though he married several wives and took concubines. At the age of fifty, he went to the Jing'an Temple to burn joss sticks before the Goddess of Mercy, praying to her for a child. On August 15 of that same year, one of his wives unexpectedly gave birth to a baby boy. He was very happy, thinking this was granted by god, really mysteriously. Therefore he named his son Li Xuan (Li the Mysterious).

Fifteen years later Li Xuan was already a bright young man. One day Li Xuan went with a servant to the country to enjoy the beautiful flowers and willows. Delighted and carefree, they came upon the Jing'an Temple. It was on the same day the Goddess of Mercy was invited by Lord Lao Zi to attend Laoshan Mountain to enjoy peach blossoms. On the way to her destination, she noticed a handsome lad walking along in a manner as shifting clouds. His familiar appearance reminded her that he was just one of her attendants who had been sent to the world for punishment fifteen years previously. At the moment she remembered when Squire Li went to the temple to pray. She regretted granting him the son he expected. Thereupon, she pointed to Li Xuan, then stepped away. All of a sudden, Li Xuan slipped and fell down into the ravine and lost consciousness. Accompanied by servants, his parents rushed to the spot. They called their son's name repeatedly. However, he never came to. Actually, it was because of being given a few pointers from the Goddess, that Li Xuan's soul had already gone with her to Heaven. And what remained was only his body.

After returning to the Heavenly Palace, Li Xuan, with the help of the Goddess of Mercy, worked diligently in cultivation of Taoism. But he still thought of his parents and looked for an opportunity to return to earth. No one knew how many years had passed. One day, during Mid-Autumn Festival (fifteenth day of the eighth lunar month), when the Goddess of Mercy was invited by the Queen Mother of the West to enjoy the festive occasion, Li Xuan returned to earth to look for his body. He had stealthily drunk the holy water prepared by the Goddess, so he rode clouds and reached the site of his original home, where what he saw was a tract of ruins dotted with a few tombs.

Since Li Xuan's soul left his body, several centuries had passed. Through disasters and wars, his dwelling was in ruins and his parents had died long ago. Of course, his body had disappeared, too. In spite of all this, Li Xuan was not willing to return to Heaven. Day in and day out, he kept wandering in the sky.

One day he discovered a beggar who had died of starvation lying in a dilapidated temple at the foot of a mountain. Instantly he attached his soul to the dead body without considering how ugly the ragged beggar's appearance was—dishevelled hair, dirty face, and lame in one leg.

Han Zhongli

According to *Dong You Ji* (*Notes on Travel in the East*) and some other legends, Han Zhongli was a general of the Han Dynasty named Zhongli Quan, so he was popularly called Han Zhongli. Enlightened by Li Tieguai, he went to the mountains to cultivate himself according to the tenets of Taoism. There he killed a tiger with a flying sword and helped poor people with money by touching a stone and turning it into gold. Finally, he and his brother Jianyue became immortal and went to Heaven. No clue about his background has been found in historical materials. However, by a coincidence, there was a general named Zhongli Mei in the early years of the Han Dynasty. Based on this, some history fabricators say Han Zhongli was just Zhongli Mei.

Zhang Guolao

Zhang Guolao is a historical figure. In the Tang Dynasty there was a Taoist by that name. (The character, *Lao*, means old and respected in Chinese.)

Of the eight celestials, Zhang Guolao surpassed the others in magical power. Anecdotes on his curious deeds have been popular for ages. It is said that he rode a white donkey which could cover thousands of kilometres a day. When taking rest, Zhang folded it like a sheet of paper and placed it in a small box. Whenever he wanted to ride it, he spewed it with water, and turned it into a real donkey.

According to legend, Zhang Guolao was a sorcerer of the Tang Dynasty, living in seclusion in the

Zhongtiao Mountains. Unwilling to reveal his origin and life experience, he only said that he was born four thousand years ago, in the time under the reign of the legendary Emperor Yao and later served as a high official. Another story tells that he refused orders from Emperor Taizong and Emperor Gaozong of the Tang Dynasty for an audience in the imperial palace, and that when Empress Wu Zetian (r. 690-705) sent an official to summon him, he pretended to be dead and laid down on the ground in front of the temple gate. Soon after lying down, worms were seen wriggling out of his body, indicating he had been dead for some time. The envoy could do nothing but to report this to the empress. As soon as the envoy left, Zhang Guolao got up and promptly left for the mountains in Hengzhou, where he lived as a hermit.

In the twenty-first year of Kaiyuan under the reign of Emperor Xuanzong (685-762), an envoy was sent to call Zhang Guolao to serve the court. Considering it the proper time for him to display his talents, he responded happily. When the emperor found that he looked too old and not like an immortal, he immediately pulled out a few hairs and knocked out his own teeth. His acts scared the emperor, who ordered him to take a rest in a bedroom. When he came out to have an audience with the emperor, he appeared to be a man of fifty with black hair and white teeth. One day when Emperor Xuanzong ordered his cook to kill a deer for eating, Zhang Guolao said, "This is a thousand-year-old celestial deer. When I followed Emperor Wudi to go hunting in the imperial park, it was captured alive. Wudi released it after tying a copper sign to its left antler." Now when Emperor Xuanzong went to look at the animal, sure enough, he found a copper tag with illegible characters attached to its antler. It was really an antique. And this further convinced the emperor that Zhang Guolao was a celestial being. Actually, this kind of trick had been played by a sorcerer, Shao Weng, before Emperor Wudi of the Han Dynasty. He first wrote the two characters "*Tian Shu*" (meaning "heavenly book") on a piece of silk and made an ox swallow it. Then he told the emperor that the ox had a heavenly book in its stomach and advised him to cut its belly open and take the book out. As a wise emperor, Wudi saw through this fraud. But Emperor Xuanzong had blind faith in ghosts and gods, so he was easily fooled by Zhang Guolao.

To deceive Emperor Xuanzong, Zhang Guolao hired several people as helpers and put them around the emperor. One day, the emperor ordered a wizard, who was able to see ghosts, to find where Guolao was. After pretending to look for him here and there, the wizard reported that he could not see him. In fact, Zhang Guolao was sitting before the wizard. This was therefore interpreted that Zhang Guolao was a real celestial, because a wizard could perceive only ghosts, but not gods. On another occasion, Zhang Guolao worked together with a Taoist called Ye Jingneng to make a fool of the emperor. When the emperor asked Ye when Zhang Guolao was born, Ye answered, "I know it. But I would be killed if I tell you the truth. Suppose I must do so, I have to ask for Your Majesty's favour to intercede with Zhang Guolao for me with bare head and feet. Only by so doing, can I save my life." After the emperor gave his promise, Ye said, "Zhang Guolao was a spirit of a white bat when earth was first separated from heaven." Then he died with his eyes, ears, nostrils and mouth bleeding. The emperor did as Ye requested. Pretending to be serious, Zhang Guolao remarked, "That fellow is so gossipy and meddlesome that he must be punished. Otherwise, nature's mystery would be revealed." After the emperor put in more good words for Ye, Zhang spewed Ye's body with a mouthful of water. Strange to say, the dead was brought back to life.

The emperor was not only spellbound by this fraud, but he also admired Zhang Guolao. He even planned to have his daughter, Princess Yu Zhen, marry him. In addition, he offered Zhang an important post and conferred on him the title of court academician. Zhang was interested in high position and handsome salary, but he dared not marry the princess. This was because his fraud would be exposed if he were to live with her. Actually, it would be impossible to avoid people knowing if he had a long stay in the imperial palace. For this reason, he resigned his office under the pretext of being too old and in poor health after enjoying a period of luxurious life and making great wealth. At the beginning of the Tianbao period, Emperor Xuanzong again sent an envoy to call him back to the court. He refused by pretending to be dead and instructing his disciples to have his body buried. When the envoy opened the coffin, he found it was empty. This kind of "empty-coffin stratagem" had been repeatedly described in the classical novels of Western Europe. But, in the Tang Dynasty when legends about gods were popular, Taoists regarded this as ascending to Heaven and becoming immortal. So, Zhang Guolao was always considered a celestial. According to *New Records of the Tang Dynasty*, after Zhang Guolao died, Emperor Xuanzong built a Qixia Temple in Puwu County in memory of him.

He Xiangu

He Xiangu was the only female of the Eight Immortals. As opinions on her origin varied, no unanimous conclusion was made.

According to *Ji Xian Zhuan* (*Collected Stories of Celestials*) by Zeng Zao of the Song Dynasty, He Xiangu, also named He Qiong, was a Taoist nun of Yongzhou in the Tang Dynasty. One day in her childhood, accompanied by a friend she went deep in the mountains to gather medicinal herbs. On the way she wandered away from her companion and met a stranger, who offered her a peach. After eating it she became so magical that she could predict the future. Local people said, "She must be instructed by gods and come to benefit her native land." Thereupon, they set up a building to house her and called her He Xiangu (He the Fairy Maiden).

According to *Xu Tong Kao* (*Sequel to a Comprehensive Study of Civilization*), He Xiangu was born at Yunmuxi in Zengcheng County, Guangdong Province during the reign of Empress Wu Zetian of the Tang Dynasty. In her childhood her family was so poor that she gave her grain ration to her mother. At age fifteen, she met a celestial in a dream, who told her to eat mica powder to allay her hunger. She did as he said. Several years later, she felt her movement was as nimble as a flying swallow. Then she decided not to marry. From then on, she set out early in the morning and came back at dusk with fresh fruits gathered in the mountains for her mother. Because she didn't eat cereals all year round, she spoke in an abnormal way. As the news reached the court, Empress Wu Zetian summoned her to the imperial palace. On her way to the capital she rose to the sky and became a celestial. Afterwards, some people in Magutan saw her standing amid colourful clouds. During the Dali period (766-780), she was seen in Xiaoshilou of Guangzhou.

According to *Luofu Records* by Chen Lian of the Ming Dynasty, He Xiangu came from Lingling of

Hunan in the Tang Dynasty. When she was born she had six hairs on the top of her head. At the age of thirteen, she often went to the mountains to collect tea. One day, she encountered the celestial Lü Dongbin who gave her a peach and told her, "You will become immortal if you eat it." She did as he said. Consequently, she never felt hungry and thirsty. In addition, she could tell people's good and bad fortune.

Annals of Anqing Prefecture sounds even more fantastic when it says that He Xiangu was borne by a deer and was brought up by a Taoist named He.

Another tale said that He Xiangu was actually the female celestial Zhao who attained enlightenment and immortality with the help of Lü Dongbin. She was surnamed He because she always held lotus in hand (*he* meaning "lotus" in Chinese). Still another tale said that He Xiangu was the incarnate of a person called Xu Shengchen who attached her soul to a dead woman named He.

Of all the legends about He Xiangu, the following is the most interesting:

Gao Lishe (684-762) was a favourite of Emperor Xuanzong of the Tang Dynasty. Formerly, he served as a general. Later, he was captured in a battle, then castrated and became a eunuch. Now he set out for Longzhou (today's Luoding) in Guangdong to escort his mother to Chang'an. After his arrival in Guangdong, he casually told the local elders and brethren about the court affairs on various occasions, including the information of the emperor's worship of Taoism and celestials. As the news reached the ears of the old man He Tai, who was living in Chungangli, Zengcheng County, he pondered the matter and an idea came to his mind.

Originally, during the Kaiyao period (681-682) of Emperor Gaozong, He Tai had a daughter, He Erniang, who was clever and pretty early in her childhood. At eighteen, she looked even more beautiful. Old He intended to marry her to a young man from a rich family, but she was reluctant to do so. On the eve of the marriage, she disappeared. A few days later, a pair of shoes were found at the edge of a well. They belonged to He Erniang.

He Tai and others of the family tried unsuccessfully to retrieve the body from the well. Gossips said, "Old fellow He forced his daughter to escape from home." He Tai was embarrassed, but he suffered in silence. Afterwards, an idea occurred to him when he heard that the emperor in Chang'an wanted to become immortal. He ordered his family to prepare a good meal, including dishes of fish and bean curd, and rice wine to entertain a few scholars of his acquaintance. The guests were happy and drank to their hearts' content. When they asked the host what he wanted them to do, He Tai told them about his plan.

This entertainment accomplished its purpose. A short time later, a Taoist named Cai Taiyi (Cai the Great Monad) came to Chungangli, the area where

He Tai dwelled, to inquire about He's address. He told the local people, "As a Taoist priest roaming in the Luofu Mountains, I saw a colourful cloud lingering in the sky over Magutan, on which a goddess stood, wearing a phoenix coronet and a multihued cape. She told me she was He Xiangu and asked me to tell the family of He Tai in Chungangli of Zengcheng County to keep the shoes she left at the edge of the well. When I was kneeling before her, the colourful cloud shifted away from Magutan and carried the female celestial up to Heaven."

After hearing what the Taoist priest said, some people believed, and some doubted. But the family of He Tai responded in a different way. They decorated their houses with lanterns and coloured streamers and entertained relatives and friends on a grand scale, claiming their daughter Erniang had become immortal. After lots of wine, the scholars reminded each other, "From now on, we should call He's daughter He Xiangu (He the Fairy Maiden) instead of He Erniang. Otherwise, we would offend the immortal." Then they added seriously, "Each line of the poems He Xiangu asked Cai the Great Monad to bring back has its celestial charm. These masterpieces could only be created by immortals."

The story provides still another legend. He Xiangu was said to live in Hedong Village by the Jiushui River north of Mt. Laoshan in Qingdao, Shandong Province. Called He Hua (Lotus Flower), she had a father, mother, brother and sister-in-law.

One day in June, He Hua went with her newly-married sister-in-law to wash clothes by the beach. Suddenly He Hua saw a large fresh peach floating on the water. She asked her sister-in-law to look at it. Casually casting a glance, the sister-in-law said it was but a lump of donkey dung. Feeling wronged, He Hua picked up the peach and asked her sister-in-law to sample it. Her sister-in-law still insisted that it was donkey dung. He Hua said to herself, "Since she thinks so, I'll eat it." After eating the peach, she felt comfortable all over, and both her hearing and eyesight became sharper.

At this moment, the sky clouded over and a rainstorm struck amid the rumble of thunder. He Hua and her sister-in-law snatched the laundry and rushed home. After entering the house, the sister-in-law was soaked through, but He Hua was not wet. "How can you still be dry?" the sister-in-law asked.

"I chose to go through the crevices of the rain, so I could keep dry, while you just ran in the down-pour blindly. You could not avoid being drenched," He Hua responded.

"Simply nonsense! You don't have a magic eye, so how can you find crevices in the heavy rain!" the sister-in-law argued.

"If you don't believe, leave it at that," said He Hua.

The news about how He Hua ate the peach picked up from the water and how she avoided being soaked in a rainstorm quickly spread. People said, "The peach must be a celestial fruit. When He ate it, she received magic eyes and a magic body, so she could be rainproof." In the spring, when it was time for sowing, villagers came to ask her, "What kind of crops would bring in a good harvest this year?" She answered: "Those with drooping heads are the most suitable. You'd better grow them as much as you can." The villagers did not know the meaning of the words "drooping heads" at that time. But when autumn came, those who had grown millet brought in bumper harvests. Then people understood what "drooping heads" meant.

Early in the summer of the next year, He Hua began reaping wheat from her fields on the mountain slope. But it was about ten days ahead of the regular harvest time so the villagers ridiculed her and called her crazy. Hearing this, He Hua's father hurried to the field to punish her. To avoid being beaten, He Hua ran away to the mountains. Meanwhile, the old man tied all the reaped wheat into bundles and brought them home. That night, a heavy rainstorm hit the area and washed away all the wheat in the fields except that reaped by He Hua. This disaster made He Hua's father and the villagers realize why He Hua reaped the wheat ahead of schedule and regretted they had not followed her example.

The following day, the sun came out, but He Hua did not return home so the villagers went to the mountains to look for her. Many days of search covered countless ridges, mountain streams and caves without a trace of He Hua. One evening, a few people came upon a stone cave in the side of a mountain. When they entered it, they found He Hua sitting in a lotus-shaped basin with half-closed eyes and palms together. They called her but she did not answer. They dragged her but she did not move. When her parents, brother and sister-in-law came to take her home, she still made no response. Her father felt he had no alternative but to collect a bundle of firewood and place it at the cave's opening and smoke her out.

Unexpectedly, a flash of red ray coming out of the cave penetrated the smoke and flames and rose in the air. Standing on the top of the smoke was He Hua. She held a red lotus in one hand and kept waving farewell to her parents and villagers. Then she flew to the fairyland of Penglai to meet the other seven celestials. She has been remembered and respected ever since. Because her name was He Hua, she was addressed as He the Fairy Maiden.

Lan Caihe

Lan Caihe was a real figure in history. Born in the late Tang Dynasty, he was a vagrant when growing up, choosing to live on alms. Always in a blue ragged garment, singing as he went begging. Nothing supernatural could be found from his careless and casual manners. How did he happen to become a celestial? There were different versions of it.

According to *Xu Xian Zhuan* (*Sequel to the Biographies of Immortals*) by Shen Fen of the Southern Tang Dynasty, no one knew when Lan Caihe was born or where he came from. One foot in a shoe and the other bare, with clappers in hand, he always wore a blue tattered garment and begged for his food in busy streets. He always sang when drunk, travelling far and wide. One day as he was drinking in a wineshop, melodious music suddenly sounded in the air. In a twinkling he was seen ascending into the sky.

The record about Lan Caihe from *Que Qian's Encyclopedia* was similar to what was told above. But he was not unknown. It said, for example, "Lan Caihe was a hermit of the late Tang Dynasty. Wearing cotton-padded clothes in summer and sleeping on ice or snow in winter, he frequently sang while wandering about the streets of Chang'an, with a basket in hand. Some had seen him in childhood, but they found he was still the same in appearance when they were growing old. Later, as he was drinking in a restaurant, rosy clouds were hovering above it. As soon as he finished drinking, he rode a crane into the sky. Suddenly his shoes, clothes, waistband, and clappers were thrown down from the clouds. And, after a while, all of these articles disappeared."

According to *Taiping Miscellany*, Lan Caihe, unconventional and unrestrained, was fond of travelling. As a rule, he wore a cotton-padded garment in summer and slept on snow-covered ground in winter. When lying on the snow, the air he exhaled was hot as steam. When singing and walking in the streets, he was always followed by a number of people, old and young. Whenever questioned, he would set the audience laughing with his response. When given cash, he ran through them with a string and pulled them along with him. When some cash was lost, he did not mind. Sometimes, he gave the money to help the poor, or to pay the wineshop for his drinks. To beg for food, he would sing while beating time with feet and clappers, a way popular in the Tang Dynasty. Words of his ballads were mostly of admonition, setting people thinking. Because of his peculiar behaviour, he gradually became well-known.

According to a Yuan Dynasty play, he was a musician, and Lan Caihe was his stage name. Born in Lujiang in the late Tang Dynasty, he was originally called Xu Jian and styled himself Jie Shi. Because he offended local authorities, he was punished severely. Later, he was enlightened by Han Zhongli and became a supernatural being.

Another reason Lan Caihe was described as a celestial was connected with Taoism. His miraculous deeds deeply impressed the people. So he was made a god. More legends similar to the above are found in Taoist works.

The book, *Shen Xian Zhuan* (*Stories About Celes-*

tials), tells about the time Lan Caihe was drinking in Haoliang Wineshop and met an old man, who was tall and strong and had a sonorous voice, and was led by him onto a bridge where he was asked to throw himself into the turbulent flow. From then on, he took Han Zhongli as his teacher until finally he achieved the Tao (the Way) and turned immortal.

The group of the Eight Immortals was probably formed in the Yuan Dynasty. In the play "Lan Caihe" by a playwright of that time, his image was portrayed as a male character. But in the play "Eight Immortals Celebrating Birthdays" presented in the Ming Dynasty, Lan Caihe appeared as a fairy maiden, and was worshipped by devout Taoist converts.

Lü Dongbin

Lü Dongbin, or Lü Chunyang, was respected everywhere as Master Lü and was worshipped in temples of many places. The Chunyang Temple at Shuzhugang in Guangzhou, Chunyang Hall on Mt. Emei in Sichuan, and Yongle Temple in Ruicheng of Shanxi were all built to enshrine him. Many feudal rulers even paid him higher tribute. Quan Zhen Dao, a school of Taoism, respectfully called him one of the five venerable founders in the north, and set the fourteenth day of the fourth month of the lunar year to be his birthday for a memorial ceremony on a grand scale.

Of the legends about the Eight Immortals, those about Lü Dongbin were most numerous. On the questions of his name and native place, there were several versions. One contends he came from Hezhong Prefecture (today's Yongji County in Shanxi Province) in the Tang Dynasty. He had twice failed in the highest imperial examinations. Disappointed, he led a vagabond life. Then peasant uprisings broke . out in parts of the country. The most powerful rebellious army headed by Huang Chao directly menaced the imperial court. Because of the upheaval, Lü Dongbin lived in seclusion in the Zhongnan Mountains and styled himself Taoist Hui. As war spread to the place where he lived, he moved to Mt. Emei in Sichuan, first secluded in Zizhi Cave and then in Qianren Cave to practise Taoism.

Another version has Lü Dongbin coming from Jingzhao (northwest of today's Chang'an County in Shaanxi) in the Tang Dynasty. After repeated failures in the highest imperial examinations, he gave up hope and intended to commit suicide. At this crucial moment, he happened to meet Han Zhongli, who made him sleep in the cave while cooking a pot of millet beside him. Lü dreamed that he was given the title of Zhuangyuan (number one scholar who came first in the highest imperial examinations) and promoted to a high position, and that he married a girl from a rich and powerful family and soon afterwards they had children. Later he was appointed prime minister, holding state power and enjoying a life of luxury for ten years. Then one day, when the emperor lost his temper, he was removed from office, his house searched, and his property confiscated. In addition, his wife and daughter were enslaved, his son and son-in-law, both also ranking officials, were jailed, and he was banished. When he got to the slope of the Zhongnan Mountains and was about to take his own life by throwing himself down from a crag, he woke up, finding Han Zhongli fanning the stove, smiling. Lü Dongbin was disillusioned with the mortal world and followed Han Zhongli to practise Taoism.

One version said Lü Dongbin was a native of Yongle (now Yongluo) County in Shanxi. After his second failure in the highest imperial examinations, he became a loafer, travelling far and wide. At the age of sixty-four, he encountered Han Zhongli, who explained the secret of practising Taoism to him. Then he became a priest and lived in seclusion in the Zhongnan Mountains. In another version, he was born in the late Tang Dynasty. He failed several times in the highest imperial examinations. One day on the way to Huashan Mountain he met Han Zhongli, who taught him how to make immortality pills. Afterwards, he toured the country. Apart from this, he was noted for other unusual deeds including killing flood dragons in the Yangtze and Huai rivers, playing with cranes in Yueyang, and getting drunk at an inn.

Still another version has Lü Dongbin coming from Yongle Town of Ruicheng in Shanxi. His ancestors had been officials in the Sui and Tang dynasties. In the first year of the Baoli period (A.D. 823), he passed as a successful candidate in the highest imperial examinations. After serving as magistrate of two counties for a few years, he resigned office and went to the Jiufeng Mountains to practise Taoism. Before leaving home, he distributed all his property to the poor people. He climbed the mountains and lived in a cave opposite to the one occupied by his wife. It was in the mountains that Lü Dongbin met Han Zhongli, who gave him immortality pills and secret writings and taught him how to employ the double-edged sword. Through a period of practising Taoism he became a supernatural being. Then he went down the mountains and roamed all over the country. Wherever he went, he gave patients free medical treatment. Once he became intoxicated from drinking tortoise-snake liquor at Yueyang Tower. Later, a structure was set up at the site to mark the event. The earliest legend about him spread around the area of Yuezhou in the Northern Song Dynasty.

Lü Dongbin's position in Taoism was also the highest among the Eight Immortals. During the Yuan and Ming dynasties he was given the title of Lord Chunyang. Of the Taoist temples, those built for him attracted the largest number of pilgrims till modern times. If we only cast a glance over the records on the origin of the Eight Immortals, we will find that Lü Dongbin was the key figure despite the fact that he was middle-aged and not the most capable in practising Taoism.

Lü Dongbin had the human touch. In addition to travelling across the land, treating diseases, mediating disputes for the common people, and eliminating evils and demons, he was good-natured and unrestrained in manner, and was loved by the masses. When Taoism was promoted by the rulers of the Yuan and Ming dynasties, Lü Dongbin was further worshipped.

Han Xiangzi

The story about Han Xiangzi (or Han Xiang) was first told in the book *Youyang Zazhu* by Duan Chengshi of the Tang Dynasty. He was said to be the nephew of Han Yu, a great writer of the Tang Dynasty. He was unconventional and uninhibited in childhood, reluctant to study, fond of drinking, and loved to associate with Buddhist monks and Taoist priests. Afterwards, he learned about Taoism from Lü Dongbin and finally became immortal. To enlighten his uncle Han Yu to follow him, he distinguished himself on one occasion when Han Yu gave a banquet. First, he poured each guest a glass of wine with a tiny flagon which was only one inch in diameter. Then he spewed a mouthful of water into a clay basin. All of a sudden a bud broke through the soil. And in a little while it grew up as a tree peony with a green blossom as large as a bowl.

According to the *Genealogical Table of Prime Ministers in the Tang Dynasty*, Han Yu really had a grand nephew (not nephew) named Han Xiang. In the third year of the Changqing period (A.D. 823) under the reign of Emperor Muzong, Han Xiang was chosen as a successful candidate in the highest imperial examinations. Later he ranked among senior officials. His main interest seemed to be achieving high position and handsome salary.

One reason Han Xiangzi was able to become immortal was probably because of his gardening activities. The story about his growing peony was recorded in a book by Duan Chengshi who was his contemporary. It was said that he dug holes around peony trees deep to their roots and spread purple ore powder into them. Then he tended them carefully every morning and night. About seven days later, he filled all the holes with earth. Strangely, the plants bloomed soon. The flowers came in white, red, and green, and each had fourteen characters on its petals.

Another reason for Han Xiangzi's becoming immortal might be connected with the popularization of Taoist thought in the Tang Dynasty. To prove that Taoists became supernatural beings through practising Taoism was not legend, it was necessary to cite some "real people and real deeds" as examples for propaganda. Han Xiangzi was just the right character. Based on the fact that he was Han Yu's grand nephew and a skillful peony grower, mysterious tales about him were created and had him deified. For instance, the story on his growing peony was exaggerated by *Han Xian Zhuan* (*Biography of Immortal Han*) to be "growing fiery lotus in a fiery pot." He was also said to be a hero in helping Han Yu subdue crocodiles on the basis of the noted writer's article about offering sacrifices to the creature.

Since the Yuan and Ming dynasties, Han Xiangzi has been described in many books and novels, and even presented on stage. People said that he had followed Lü Dongbin to practise Taoism, so he was included among the Eight Immortals.

Cao Guojiu

Cao Guojiu (Cao the Imperial Uncle), originally named Cao Yi, was believed to be the brother of Empress Dowager Cao of the Song Dynasty.

In mythology, Cao Guojiu was also named Cao Jingxiu. He was kind and honest in nature, fond of leading a peaceful and quiet life, and reluctant to seek wealth and position. His brother Cao Jingzhi was arrogant, wilful and unlawful. To avoid being involved in trouble, he distributed his property to the poor, then went deep in the mountains to live in seclusion and devote himself to the practice of Taoism.

One day he came to the bank of the Yellow River. Proud of being the Imperial Uncle, he called two boatmen to ferry him across the river. But the boatmen refused. They asked him to pay in advance. He had no money, so he produced a gold plate granted by the emperor to show his identity. Unexpectedly, the boatmen said, "Since you want to cultivate yourself in light of Taoism, why do you frighten us with such a thing? Isn't this nonsense!" These remarks convinced him that he was wrong. Without hesitation he threw the gold plate into the river. Having looked at the boatmen carefully, he came to recognize that they were the immortals Han Zhongli and Lü Dongbin.

"They say you've been concentrating on seeking a way of becoming immortal. What is it?" asked Lü.

"It is the Way of Taoism," answered Cao.

"Where is the Way of Taoism?" asked Lü.

Cao pointed to the heavens.

"Where is Heaven?" Lü pursued.

Cao pointed to his heart.

Now, Han Zhongli smiled, "Heart is Heaven, and Heaven is the Way. You yourself have already got it!"

As Han Zhongli and Lü Dongbin burst into laughter, Cao Guojiu prostrated himself before them and asked to be their disciple. Lü Dongbin produced a pair of jade boards and threw them into the river.

He and Cao respectively stepped on one of them while Han Zhongli was stepping on a palm fan. They were all ferried to the opposite bank. From then on, the pair of jade boards were kept by Cao Guojiu as his talisman.

According to another legend, Cao Guojiu was originally named Cao Yi, who styled himself Gongbai. His grandfather Cao Bing was the Prince of Han and his sister was the empress (the Song emperor Renzong's wife). In his childhood he was handsome and quiet, so he was loved by the emperor and empress. He was granted a gold plate by the emperor when he asked to become a monk. As he came to the bank of the Yellow River and found no money to pay the boatmen, he had to leave the gold plate as a pledge. Seeing his embarrassment, Lü Dongbin gave him a warning. This made him understand the Way and how to free himself from the world of mortals.

Cao Yi was a dandy in private life. Amiable and easy of approach, he was good at music, chess and archery, and fond of composing poems. He had refined manners, but he was worldly-wise and played safe, and accomplished nothing. Whenever he was out of court, he never talked about politics. In officialdom he tried his best not to offend anybody. So he was appreciated by Emperor Shenzong and praised as a good official. During years of political turbulence, some honest and upright officials were ignored. But he was constantly esteemed and welcomed in official circles. He died at age seventy-two. After his death, he was posthumously conferred the title of Tai Shi (Imperial Tutor) and the Prince of Yi.

Cao Yi's philosophy of life—holding oneself aloof from the world—was consistent with a Taoist concept of human conduct—letting things take their own course. At the same time, the goal a Taoist pursued was to live a happy life on earth and ascend to Heaven and become immortal after death. So Cao Yi was the ideal figure appreciated by Taoists and was therefore publicized by them as a supernatural being.

In Yuan Dynasty drama Cao Guojiu was presented as one of the Eight Immortals, and more similar records about him appeared in the succeeding Ming Dynasty.

GOD OF THE YELLOW RIVER

River God, the God of the Yellow River, was the most influential of ancient China's water gods. The Yellow River is the second largest river in China, measuring 5,464 kilometres long. It is the birthplace of Chinese civilization. Holding a memorial ceremony for the River God indicated the important position of the Yellow River in the hearts of the Chinese people.

At first, the River God was worshipped in different areas. In the sixteenth century B.C. when the Shang Dynasty was founded, enshrining the River God became popular and this resulted in the establishment of many temples for him. During the Spring and Autumn (770-476 B.C.) and Warring States (475-221 B.C.) periods, activities of worshipping the River God were livened up in various places. The River God came to be known as He Bo (River Uncle).

Since the Qin and Han dynasties, worshipping He Bo had been regarded as a state memorial ceremony. In the Tang Dynasty and after, he was conferred the title of duke or prince. After the introduction of Buddhism into China, the integration of the

God of the Yellow River

Dragon King in Buddhist scriptures with the Dragon God in folk tales became a symbol of the River God. There were several River Gods described in Chinese mythology. Now two of them are introduced here.

He Bo

He Bo (River Uncle) was named Feng Yi. He was also known as Bing Yi or Wu Yi. According to historical data, Feng Yi came from Tongxiang in Huayin County. After taking some medicine called Bashi, he became the River God, He Bo. According to legend, Feng Yi was drowned while crossing a river one day in August and the Heavenly Emperor named him He Bo. Another version describes He Bo as a distinguished young man with a fair face and a slender figure. When he showed his true features, the lower part of his body resembled a fish tail. He frequently roamed on nine rivers with female celestials by riding a vehicle made of lotus leaves, which was pulled by a dragon-like creature.

According to *Shui Jing Zhu* (*Commentary on the "Waterways Classic"*), the custom of marrying a girl to He Bo had been in existence in the area of Ye (today's Linzhang County, Hebei Province) within the domain of the State of Wei during the Warring States Period. This "marriage" was arranged by the local authorities. Every year people were cheated this way and a great amount of their wealth flowed into the pockets of those in power. As a rule, when the date for "marriage" was approaching, witches were sent to "visit" families. When they found a beautiful girl, they would say, "She should be married to He Bo." After giving the family some money as bride-price, they put the girl by force on a decorated bed on which was spread a mat of woven split bamboo. Carried by nine strong men to the river bank, the girl was thrown into the water. In view of this terrible situation, most families with girls escaped from this area. The masses were strongly against this evil custom, but they dared not oppose it openly for fear that their fields would be flooded once He Bo became angry.

Later, Ximen Bao was appointed magistrate of Ye County. When he found out how the people suffered from this custom, he abolished it. Working out a clever device, he got the witches and officials in charge of marrying girls to He Bo thrown into the Zhang River. People there then were liberated from that evil custom.

Here is another story about He Bo: During the Spring and Autumn Period, there was a warrior named Tantai Mieming, who came from Wucheng (southwest of today's Feixian County in Shandong Province) in the State of Lu. He was ugly in appearance but had a heart of gold. One day when he was carrying a piece of costly white jade and leaving Yanjin (north of today's Yanjin County in Henan Province) to cross the Yellow River, He Bo, who had got this information beforehand, tried to stir up trouble in an attempt to seize the precious jade. As the boat was rowed to the midstream, he first sent Great Wave God to make high waves, then ordered two flood dragons to attack and capsize the boat. Fully understanding what this meant, Tantai Mieming was undaunted. He stood at the prow and shouted at the flood dragons, "You may have my jade by appropriate means, but if you resort to force, that won't do!" As soon as he finished speaking, he drew his sword and battled against the flood dragons. After a few rounds, he killed them. Facing this unfavourable situation, Great Wave God decamped right away, and the waves calmed down. The boat arrived safely at the opposite bank. Tantai Mieming then produced the white jade and threw it into the river, saying disdainfully, "Take it away." Strangely, the jade rebounded into his hand from the water surface. He threw it in again, and it rebounded once more. This was repeated three times in succession. Why did He Bo refused to accept it? He likely realized that taking jade this way was dishonourable. Tantai Mieming then crashed the jade against a rock and swaggered off, showing that he fought not for the jade but for something more precious.

Ju Ling

Ju Ling (Giant Spirit) as a River God was first

mentioned in *Xi Jing Fu (Ode to the Western Capital)* written by Zhang Heng of the Eastern Han Dynasty.

According to a number of novels and tales in ancient times, Ju Ling was the son of Queen Mother of the West, having connection with the mythology about the creation of the world. Because he was capable of making mountains and rivers, he was worshipped as River God.

One of the stories has Ju Ling cutting through mountains to bring in water from the Yellow River.

The turn of the Yellow River near Tongguan is a well-known big bend. Here the watercourse is narrow, the flow is rapid, and the mountains along the banks are precipitous. Being stopped here by Huashan Mountain, the flow of the river from the north turns round and runs along Zhongtiao Mountain to the east.

In ancient times the Huashan and Zhongtiao mountains were linked together. When the flow of the Yellow River was stopped here by rocks, the areas around were flooded. River God Ju Ling grieved at the sight of the people suffering from floods. He decided to channel the water of the Yellow River eastward into the sea.

One day, Ju Ling went up the mountains, stripped to the waist. As he got into a deep valley, he changed himself into a giant by a shake of his body. He turned to face the east, stretching his hands to push against two peaks. The peaks were given a good shaking. After a rest, he stretched his legs and rubbed his arms for a while. All of a sudden, his fingers and toes became dozens of feet long.

Ju Ling drew a deep breath and mustered all his energy. Following an earth-shaking roar, he pushed the two peaks towards either side with his big palms. The rock cracked. At this moment, he hurried to prop Huashan Mountain with his hands while stretching out his leg to move Zhongtiao Mountain northward. This resulted in a gorge through which the water of the Yellow River kept running eastward along the foot of Zhongtiao Mountain.

Now, on the blackish cliff on the right of the eastern peak of Huashan Mountain, one can see five coulourful belts resembling human fingers. On the slope of Shouyang Mountain, a footprint about three inches deep and four feet long is seen. Beside it, three engraved characters read, "Ju Ling's Footprint."

"Roaring with rage, Ju Ling pushed two peaks apart, and the rapid current of the Yellow River was channelled into the East Sea," are the lines from a poem by Li Bai, a great poet of the Tang Dynasty.

THE MOON GODDESS

The Moon Goddess in mythology generally referred to Chang'e, wife of Hou Yi. She was said to have taken on the sly the elixir presented to her husband by Queen Mother of the West, then flew to the moon and became a fairy. For ages she has been worshipped by the people as the Moon Goddess, especially on the night of the Mid-Autumn Festival (fifteenth day of the eighth lunar month).

According to legend, Chang'e and Hou Yi were celestials. Because people on earth could not stand the heat radiated from the ten suns which were always simultaneously rising in the sky, the Heavenly Emperor sent Hou Yi down to the mortal world to investigate. He found the people were unable to endure such terrible heat; some were already dead, others were dying. They gathered in crowds, shouting and cheering, and demanding that Hou Yi eliminate the scourge. He immediately shot down nine suns with arrows. But the nine suns were the sons of the Heavenly Emperor. Furious, he banished Hou Yi and his wife to the mortal world. Chang'e was a narrow-minded woman and she complained about their punishment.

月光

The Moon Goddess

One day, Chang'e said to her husband, "I'm complaining of nothing else but of your rash action, your shooting the sons of the Heavenly Emperor. Because of this, we are relegated to be mortals. As mortals, we will die. After death, we will get into hell and live together with ghosts, and lead a miserable life. What a terrible thing!"

"Yes, I know," responded Hou Yi. "I don't want to go to hell either. But, what can I do?"

Thinking a little while, Chang'e remarked, "They say in the Kunlun Mountains lives Queen Mother of the West."

"Yes, the Queen Mother lives there."

"She has immortal pills."

"Right, she has that magic medicine." Hou Yi added, "One would become immortal by taking it. Why didn't I think of it? I'm going tomorrow to go to the Queen Mother to ask for the elixir."

After being banished to the mortal world, Cheng'e always wore a worried frown. Now she beamed, "Go ahead, I hope you will achieve your wish; I'll wait for you." Taking food as well as a bow and arrows, Hou Yi set out for the Kunlun Mountains early the next morning.

The Kunlun area was the capital of the Yellow Emperor. At the foot of a mountain was an abyss with water of no buoyancy. Even a single feather would sink, let alone a ferryboat. Outside the abyss was a volcano always in eruption. Because of these natural barriers, no one had been able to get to the

Queen Mother's place for the elixir.

But now Hou Yi was the only one to succeed. With his magic strength and strong will, he broke through the water and fire barriers, and climbed the mountain. There he met the Queen Mother who was in charge of disasters, pestilence and punishment. She could take or give human life at any time.

After learning of Hou Yi's plight, the Queen Mother sympathized with him, and gave him enough elixir for two persons. She said, "This medicine is made of immortal fruit from the immortal tree which blossoms every three thousand years and fruits every six thousand years. Now, here is all the elixir I have. The dose will give two persons eternal life. If taken by one, it will take the person to Heaven to become a celestial. So you'd better keep it carefully."

Hou Yi thanked her and left the Kunlun Mountains for home. He asked his wife to look after the elixir and planned to choose a festive occasion for them to take it together. Hou Yi believed the situation in Heaven was no better than that on earth, so he did not want to return to Heaven. He would feel satisfied so long as he did not go to hell.

But Chang'e was eager to go back to Heaven. Too impatient to wait for a festival, she took all the elixir one night when her busband was not at home. Suddenly she felt as if treading on air and she flew out of the window. As shc was ascending in the sky, she began to worry what the fairy maidens would

219

say when she returned to Heaven. "They would think I've abandoned my husband. It seems proper for me to go to the moon for a brief stay."

She decided to fly straight to the moon. When she got there, she found a cold and deserted place where there was nothing except a white rabbit, a toad, and an osmanthus tree. Many years later, a man named Wu Gang was banished to the moon to fell the osmanthus tree for his fault in seeking the way of being immortal. The tree measured over 150 metres high. Each cut he made with an ax invariably healed at once. So it could never be cut down.

Chang'e felt disappointed. However, she had no choice but to stay. Now, she began to think of her happy family and the advantages of her husband. If she had not taken the elixir alone, she and her husband would be immortal, living together in the mortal world. She regretted what she had done and wished she could fly down to earth and apologize to her husband. But this was impossible. She had to stay on the moon forever.

That night when he came back, Hou Yi found his wife had disappeared. On the table was an empty medical kit. He knew what had happened. His heart was filled with anger, disappointment, and sorrow. The only way for him to dispel his vexation was to get his bow and arrows and ride off on his horse into the open country or to hunt in the forests. A fight against wild animals might set him free from gloom.

As for the origin of Chang'e, there were several different records in ancient books. Tales about the Moon Goddess, Moon Spirit, toad, white rabbit, osmanthus tree, and the Moon Palace also varied. According to one legend, Di Jun was the god worshipped by the clans in the east of ancient China. He had three wives—one was called E Huang, one called Xi He, who was the Sun Goddess and had ten sons. Later, nine of them were shot down by Hou Yi. The other wife was Chang'e, the Moon Goddess, who had twelve daughters, and often helped them bathe in a deserted spot in the west.

Since the invention of the astronomical telescope, people have discovered a shadow in the moon. But it is not the Guanghan (Broad Cold) Palace or the Moon Palace as legends claim. Of course, there is no Chang'e or white rabbit there. In the winter of 1970, the United States sent a spaceship to the moon. Astronauts found only a vast expanse of desert; no moon goddess.

THE THUNDER GOD

Thunder and lightning were especially worshipped by the primitives because they dramatized the mystery and power of nature. They frequently brought storms, sometimes resulting in a fire and death. The development of the psychology of this natural phenomenon—holding in awe, fear, and respect, led to the superstitious belief of thunder and the creation of the image of the Thunder God.

In mythology, the Thunder God was said to be in charge of thunder. In ancient times, his appearance was portrayed out of imagination based on the frightening rumble of thunder. Mention of the god can be found in ancient Chinese books. One said he lived in Thunder Pool. He had a green face, glaring eyes, a human head and dragon body. While beating his belly, the roll of thunder sounded. Another popular one had him resembling a monkey. Since the Spring and Autumn and the Warring States periods, the Thunder God had been given many social functions. It was thought that he could punish on behalf of Heaven, could strike vicious persons, distinguish between good and evil, and uphold justice. According to another one, a dutiful son was

The Thunder God

struck dead by lightning when he was bringing a chicken to his mother, and he then became the Thunder God, who looked like a chicken.

Still another one: Thunder God's father, Chen Gong, came from Leizhou. He had no children and earned his living by hunting. He had a miraculous dog with nine ears. The movement of its ears could foretell the number of wild animals he would catch. If one ear moved, he would catch one animal. If three or four ears moved, he would catch that number. One day, finding the nine ears of the dog moving, he felt happy, expecting to catch many. When he came to a forest, the dog suddenly turned round and picked up a huge egg. As he carried it home, the egg cracked itself and a baby boy got out of it. Both his palms were found bearing a Chinese character; the one on the left palm read *Lei* (thunder) and the one on the right read *Zhou* (prefecture). From then on, a fairy maiden came regularly to breast-feed the baby, and the local people called him the son of thunder. When he grew up, he was appointed governor of Leizhou. Later a temple was built for him and he was enshrined as the Thunder God.

According to the *Classic of Mountains and Rivers* and other books, the Thunder God often appeared in the form of an animal. The rumble of thunder, they alleged, came from the beating of celestial drums. The fabled drum and Thunder God were originally an organic whole. Afterwards, the thunder drum was regarded as a kind of instrument under the control of the Thunder God. After the Han Dynasty, the Thunder God in animal form became personalized. A legend from *Ji Shen Lu* (*A General Survey of Chinese Deities*) claims the Thunder God not only wanted to get married, but also had many relatives. His wedding ceremony was the same as that in the mortal world. With the progress of personification, people gradually held that the Thunder God might be more than one. So the author of the *Romance of the Canonized Gods*, based on the features of human nature, created the Thunder God to take charge of the Thunder Pantheon. Although the legend about the Thunder God of Leizhou and the temple built for him drew a forced analogy, the image of the Thunder God was the product of personification by later generations.

LOCAL GOD OF THE LAND

*I*n old China, whenever people made a tour in town or the countryside, they would find the Local God of the Land (also called Village God) was enshrined and worshipped by every family, and a temple had been built for him. The second day of the second lunar month was set as the birthday of the Local God. It was an occasion for celebration.

According to legend, the Local God was only a petty official administering a small area, and the scope of his function and power was narrow. He used to wear a black gauze cap and a red robe. His position was low, and he was not allowed to get into an official residence. In front of a majestic temple, he looked like just a doorkeeper. In the eyes of the common people, he was of no importance. Although regarded as the god of the household, he enjoyed no sacrificial offerings. Usually children cherished a deep affection for him, taking the statue of him as a toy. Sometimes a naughty boy would urinate on him, but he was not punished by his parents.

Another legend described the Local God as a labour hero. Breaking through brambles and thorns

Local God of the Land

and reclaiming wasteland, he had made great contributions to farm production in ancient times. From the classical book *Zuo Zhuan* (*Zuo Qiuming's Commentary on the "Spring and Autumn Annals"*), one can find this brief introduction of the Local God: "Gou Long, the son of Gong Gong, was capable of harnessing rivers and levelling soil. So he was worshipped as Local God of the land."

Gong Gong was said to be one with a human face and snake body and in charge of various trades. Once when fighting Zhuan Xu for the throne, he was defeated. Boiling with rage, he dashed against Buzhou Mountain, breaking the heavenly pillar and sky, resulting in a heavy rain.

When people first learned how to grow grain crops and other plants, the earth was still bleak and desolate. Forests here and there were haunted by snakes and fierce animals. In order to develop agriculture, part of the forests had to be felled, and the snakes and beasts of prey driven away from the cultivated land. On the other hand, it was necessary to dig canals for irrigation. Working only with stone tools was very difficult. Anyone who could increase crop production for his tribe would be regarded as a hero and gradually deified. Since Gou Long could level soil and harness rivers, he became the hero. Enshrining Gou Long as god indicated that a distinguished worker in reclaiming wasteland and cultivating the soil was esteemed by society in ancient times. The local god of the land was given more and more superstitious colour by later generations. Being presented on the stage or portrayed in a novel as somebody like a neighbourhood head in old China, was quite different from the image of Gou Long in legend.

JIANG TAIGONG—
GOD IN CHARGE OF
GRANTING TITLES TO GODS

"Jiang Taigong is here. Other gods withdraw and keep off." Thus declared Jiang Taigong at a platform after he granted titles to other gods. "Since I have offered good posts to them, I should place myself above them at least," he declared.

One god asked, "Why should you be above us in position?"

"Because your memorial tablets are placed on the floor while mine is on the beam," replied Jiang Taigong. "The beam is above the floor."

From then on, when people were building a new house, they would paste up a banner reading "Jiang Taigong is here, good luck to you" on the beam. Then they burned joss sticks and kowtowed to it, dropping cakes from the beam (custom of northern Henan), setting off firecrackers and offering sacrifices to Jiang Taigong. When a house was vacant for years, and said to be occupied by spirits or celestials, a red paper sheet with characters reading, "Jiang Taigong is here; other gods keep out of the way,"

姜太公在此

百事無禁忌

Jiang Taigong—
God in Charge of Granting Titles to Gods

could be put up on its door. This was considered an effective way of driving out monsters.

Life Story of Real Jiang Taigong

Jiang Taigong, native of Donghai in the Zhou Dynasty, was said to be a descendant of Emperor Yandi of remote ages. One of his forefathers had been in high position during the reign of Emperor Shun. Later, due to his outstanding achievements in helping Yu the Great harness rivers, he was granted the fief of Lu (west of today's Nanyang City in Henan Province) and addressed as Marquis of Lu. For this reason, Jiang Taigong was also called Lu Shang or Lu Wang. To show him respect, later generations called him Jiang Ziya. In ancient times *zi* was an honorific title for men. Afterwards, King Wen personally travelled round the country to seek talents and met Jiang Ziya by chance. "My Taigong (referring to his venerable father) longed to meet you!" he said happily. Based on this episode, Jiang Taigong was also called "Taigong Wang" (*wang* here meaning "longing for").

Jiang Taigong was a learned man and always wanted an opportunity to put his talents into practice. But under the rule of King Zhou, the last ruler of the Shang Dynasty, he was unable to realize his ambition. Most of his life was spent in obscurity and poverty. He did not have any favourable circumstances to put his abilities to good use until he was seventy years old.

Jiang heard that King Wen, chief of the Zhou Clan in the late Shang Dynasty, was amiable and easy to approach, respecting the aged and loving children, putting those able and virtuous people in important positions. Thus Jiang came to Weishui. Setting up a thatched cottage near Panxi, he made a living by fishing, while waiting for an important post by King Wen that would give full play to his knowledge in assisting the Zhou house. But, the wise ruler he kept waiting so long to meet had not yet come to invite him. His hair turned grey, and his hope seemed futile.

However, an unexpected change took place at last. One day he heard the sound of dogs, horses and people's voices coming from afar. A few minutes later, a delicate-featured man dressed up as a king came to him. Jiang was surprised, but he remained calm as usual with his years of training and self-cultivation. When told the distinguished visitor was King Wen of Zhou, who was eagerly seeking talents, he felt very happy and finally was appointed the prime minister. He carried out political and military reforms. Domestically, he put stress on developing production; externally, he deployed forces to conquer small neighbouring clans to expand territories and weaken the Shang Dynasty. With Jiang's assistance King Wen defeated Quanrong, conquered Shang Dynasty's Chongguo, and moved the capital from Qishan to Fengcheng. In his remaining years, the territory of Zhou already stretched from Mi (today's Lingtai in Gansu Province) in the west to Yu (around today's Qinyang County in Henan Province) in the east. Then Zhou further expanded its influence to the valleys of the Yangtze, Hanshui and Rushui rivers. Its political, economic and military strength greatly surpassed that of the Shang Dynasty, paving the way for the founding of the Zhou Dynasty.

But King Wen died before he realized his ambition of overthrowing Shang. His son Ji Fa, historically known as King Wu, succeeded to the throne. Assisted by Jiang, he sent troops to fight King Zhou of Shang, and carried out his father's plan for setting up the Zhou Dynasty and making Gaojing (east of today's Fengshui of Chang'an County in Shaanxi Province) the capital. The regime was called Western Zhou in history. Due to his merits in overthrowing the Shang Dynasty, Jiang was granted the area of Qi (the central and eastern parts of today's Shandong Province) as his fief, and is regarded as the founder of the state of Qi. The noted book he wrote was titled *Taigong's Art of War*.

Jiang Taigong in Legend

There are numerous legends about Jiang Taigong. One said that his parents died when he was a child and so he followed his aunt to Zhaoge, the capital of Shang. At twelve he started working as a butcher because his aunt's family needed his help. But he failed at his job and wandered away from Zhaoge. Afterwards, he met King Wen and was able to find success. Still another legend: When King Wen was imprisoned in Youli (northwest of today's Tangyin County in Henan Province), people like Shan Yisheng and Hong Tian came to Jiang Taigong for advice on how to rescue him. After putting their heads together, they went to look for beautiful girls and various kinds of treasures to present to King Zhou. The bribery led to the release of King Wen. Hearing of Jiang's wisdom and talent, King Wen offered him important posts. One legend said Jiang fished for three days and three nights without catching anything. Later a farmer taught him the way of angling. Following the advice, Jiang caught a carp. Cutting open its belly, he found a cloth roll with characters reading "Lu Wang (namely Jiang Taigong) will be granted the area of Qi as his fief."

Another legend said Jiang Taigong did not use bait during angling. So he failed to catch fish although he had angled for over fifty years. However, he caught a big carp at last. Cutting open its belly he found a tally (issued to generals as royal authorization for troop movement in ancient China) inside it. Still another legend said King Wen dreamed of the Heavenly Emperor in a black robe standing at Lingfujin Ferry with a white-haired man behind him. The Heavenly Emperor called to him: "Chang (King Wen was named Ji Chang), I am going to grant you a good teacher and assistant. His name is Wang." To express his thanks, King Wen kowtowed again and again. The aged man behind the Heavenly Emperor paid respects in the same way. It was on this night that Jiang Taigong had the same dream. Soon afterwards when meeting Jiang, King Wen asked, "Is Wang your name?"

"Yes," responded Jiang, smiling.

"It seems I have seen you somewhere," said King Wen.

After Jiang told him the exact date, King Wen suddenly saw the light, saying, "Right, right, it's just on that day that I met you." Then he went together with Jiang back to the court and offered him an important post.

Another legend has King Wen asking an official historian to practise divination for him. "Heaven would give you a good assistant," said the historian. King Wen set out for hunting on the Weishui River. There he met Jiang Taigong, who was sitting on a bundle of hay and quietly angling. After talking with him, King Wen was overjoyed. Upon returning to the capital, King Wen took Jiang as the State Tutor.

Here is another legend: After meeting King Wen, Jiang was appointed as magistrate of Guantan County. One year later, he had made remarkable achievements in his official career—production developed, people had ample food and clothing, and the general mood of society was good. One night King Wen dreamed of a slender, beautiful girl in a bright-coloured dress crying and blocking him on the way. When asked what had happened, she said, "I'm the daughter of the God of Mt. Tai and married to the son of the East Sea God Ao Guang. Now I want to go back to my husband's home, but the magistrate of Guantan won't allow me to pass through the area because my movement would be accompanied by storm. And this would spoil the local governor's reputation and bring punishment upon myself from the Heavenly Emperor for my fault. But, if I don't ask for the storm to help, I won't be able to move forward. So I am caught in a dilemma." King Wen consulted Jiang about the dream. At this moment, somebody came up to report that a storm had just swept past the border of the land under Jiang's jurisdiction. Jiang was then promoted to a higher position in charge of political and military affairs of the country.

Here is another popular story about Jiang

The one who got Jiang Taigong completely deified was Xu Zhonglin, author of the *Romance of the Canonized Gods*, in which he exaggerated the legends related to Jiang Taigong, placing him above all other gods.

After escaping from Zhaoge, Jiang Taigong came to Xiqi and lived in seclusion at Panxi near the Weihe River. There he made friends with Wu Ji, who earned his living by selling firewood. Although poor, he was kind and honest, and got along well with Jiang. In addition, he often gave firewood, edible oil and food to Jiang.

One day, Wu Ji was carrying firewood to the town for sale. When he arrived at the bustling market, a bundle of firewood suddenly slipped off his shoulder pole, and the end of the pole struck a tradesman on the head and he died on the spot.

At this moment King Wen was passing by. On learning the case, he sentenced Wu Ji to death. He drew a circle on the ground and ordered Wu to enter it, saying, "You are not allowed to go out until the end of your days." Jail was formed by drawing a circle on the ground. This news saddened Wu's mother. To rescue her son, she made a special trip to Panxi to ask for help from Jiang Taigong. Jiang knew King Wen was strict in enforcing law. But, seeing the poor old woman and her concern for Wu Ji, he thought of a scheme to help her. Following instructions, the old woman got a spade and went to the outside of the circle. Giving the spade to Wu Ji, she told him to dig three feet deep down and then make a slant upwards so as to get out. Wu Ji did as he was told and came out of the hole instead of across the circle line on the ground.

The news reached King Wen and he sent people to have Wu Ji arrested. "Why did you disobey my law and break prison?" King Wen asked.

"I didn't escape from prison," Wu Ji answered.

"Then how did you come out?"

Wu Ji told King Wen how he had acted on Jiang Taigong's advice and that he had got out from underground instead of from the circle. On hearing this, King Wen realized Jiang was a great talent. He did not lose his temper. On the contrary, he sent his son Ji Fa together with Wu Ji to find Jiang Taigong and invite him to help govern the country.

When Ji Fa and Wu Ji came to Panxi, Jiang Taigong was concentrating on fishing. He paid no heed to them, but only mumbled, "Coming is a little fish instead of a big one; the presence of a shrimp is simply fooling around."

After this rebuff, Ji Fa returned to report Jiang's words to his father. "His intention is to want me to invite him personally. Get my carriage for me."

As soon as he got to Panxi, King Wen offered greetings to Jiang Taigong and made clear to him what he wanted.

"If you want me to help promote your great cause, you must accept a request of mine," said Jiang.

"I would like to accept even one thousand requests from you so long as you come to my aid," remarked King Wen.

"Suppose you really need me, help me onto the carriage and pull me to the capital by yourself," said Jiang, smiling.

Although unhappy in heart, King Wen accepted his demand. Because he had never done physical labour before, he grew weary after covering only a short distance. "I'm tired," shouted King Wen while sitting down on the ground.

A few minutes later, he desperately pulled the carriage a little farther.

"Do you know how many steps you have taken altogether?" Jiang Taigong asked.

"I didn't count," King Wen panted.

Making a gesture by stretching out his thumb and index finger, Jiang Taigong said, "Altogether you've pulled me forward eight hundred and eight steps, so I can guarantee the rule of your dynasty to last eight hundred and eight years."

Hearing this, King Wen hurriedly stood up, intending to pull the carriage farther on.

"It's no use now," Jiang Taigong said. "The cat is already out of the bag."

This legend is also popular:

Jiang Taigong was originally a famous general of King Wen and a noted figure respected by people. He was even believed to have become a supernatural being. So anyone who wanted to drive evil spirits out of his house invariably put on the wall a poster with characters reading, "Jiang Taigong is here. All evil spirits keep off." Tradesmen going to a temple fair especially believed in Jiang Taigong. They held that every temple might have evil spirits. Since people wanted to attend a temple fair, the ghosts would go, too. Security was to be guaranteed by policemen. But putting ghosts under control could only rely on Jiang Taigong. Hence the appearance of the poster.

Jiang Taigong is a real historical figure. He was a well-known general in the founding of the Western Zhou Dynasty. Afterwards, he was worshipped as god. Legends related to him are numerous. He is the central character in the *Romance of the Canonized Gods*. In the Tang Dynasty, he was titled Prince Wucheng and regularly offered sacrifices. Temples for enshrining him were built in many parts of the country. In the eyes of the people he was on a par with Confucius. As for the custom of putting up the poster with Jiang's name to dispel evil spirits, nobody knows when it started. People probably thought that Jiang Taigong was an all-powerful general, enjoying authority to grant titles to gods, so he could terrify all evil spirits.

中国诸神由来

程曼超　编著

*

ⓒ外文出版社

（中国北京百万庄路 24 号）

邮政编码 100037

北京外文印刷厂印刷

中国国际图书贸易总公司发行

（中国北京车公庄西路 35 号）

北京邮政信箱第 399 号　邮政编码 100044

1995 年(34 开)第一版

（英）

ISBN 7 - 119 - 00030 - 6 /G·72（外）

01880

7 - E - 2900P